SQL Server Concurrency

Locking, Blocking and Row Versioning

By Kalen Delaney

First published by Simple Talk Publishing September 2012

Edited by Tony Davis
Technical Review by Benjamin Nevarez
Cover Image by Andy Martin
Typeset by Peter Woodhouse & Gower Associates

Table of Contents

About the Author

Kalen Delaney has been working with SQL Server for 25 years, and provides performance consulting services as well as advanced SQL Server training to clients around the world, using her own custom-developed curriculum. She has been a SQL Server MVP since 1993 and has been writing about SQL Server for almost as long. Kalen has spoken at dozens of technical conferences, including every US PASS conference since the organization's founding in 1999. Kalen is a contributing editor and columnist for SQL Server Magazine and the author or co-author of several of the most deeply technical books on SQL Server, including *SQL Server 2008 Internals* and the upcoming *SQL Server 2012 Internals*, both from Microsoft Press. Kalen blogs at WWW.SQLBLOG.COM and her personal website and schedule can be found at WWW.SQLSERVERINTERNALS.COM.

About the Technical Reviewer

Benjamin Nevarez is a database professional based in Los Angeles, California. He has more than 15 years' experience with relational databases, and has been working with SQL Server since version 6.5. Benjamin has been the technical editor of the previous books by Kalen Delaney, including *SQL Server 2008 Internals*, and is the author of the book, *Inside the SQL Server Query Optimizer*. He holds a Master's Degree in Computing Science and has been a speaker at several technology conferences, including the PASS Community Summit. Benjamin's blog is at HTTP://BENJAMINNEVAREZ.COM, and he can be reached at BENJAMINNEVAREZ@YAHOO.COMAIL.

Introduction

We can define concurrency as the ability of multiple sessions to access or change shared data, at the same time. The greater the number of concurrent processes that can be active without interfering with each other, the greater the concurrency of the database system and the more scalable the system will be.

Concurrency is reduced when a session that is changing data prevents other processes from reading that data, or when a session that is reading data prevents other sessions from changing that data. I'll use the terms *reading* or *accessing* to describe the impact of using the SELECT statement on our data. Concurrency is also affected when multiple sessions attempt to change the same data simultaneously and they cannot all succeed without sacrificing data consistency. I'll use the terms *modifying*, *changing* or *writing* to describe the impact of using the INSERT, UPDATE or DELETE statements on our data.

In general, database systems can take two approaches to managing concurrent data access: *pessimistic* or *optimistic*. Prior to SQL Server 2005, pessimistic concurrency was the only available model. SQL Server 2005 and later versions support both models, but pessimistic concurrency is still the default and is the recommended model until you have thoroughly tested optimistic concurrency and verified that the extra costs are worthwhile.

This book will examine the details of both concurrency models and explain what factors we must consider when comparing the relative costs on our systems. We'll also discuss concurrency concepts, such as transactions and isolation levels, that we must understand, no matter which concurrency model we're using.

Intended Audience

This book is for anyone using SQL Server as a programmer, an administrator, or even a user, who wants to understand how SQL Server manages multiple sessions, and what causes excessive blocking. It is also for those SQL Server professionals who need to know how to troubleshoot and solve blocking and deadlocking problems, and those who need to be able to compare the costs of SQL Server's two concurrency models to make the best choice for their systems and applications.

Prerequisites

This book does not assume that you're a SQL Server expert, but I do expect that you have basic technical competency and some familiarity with SQL Server. It will help if you are relatively fluent with basic SQL statements, so that you can understand simple `SELECT` statements, which will sometimes include `JOIN` operations, as well as `INSERT`, `UPDATE` and `DELETE` statements.

You should have access to a SQL Server 2008 installation, even if it is the Evaluation edition available free from Microsoft. I tested all of the code examples on SQL Server 2008, though most should work on later editions, as well as on SQL Server 2005.

My examples were all created using SQL Server Management Studio (SSMS), and formatted automatically using Red Gate's SQL Prompt tool. The latter is an optional tool, but the former is not, and I assume in the book that you know how to enter and execute queries. We will also occasionally use the SQL Server Profiler tool.

Basic Terms

Let's start with a few very basic definitions as they apply to SQL Server. I'll introduce more terms, as necessary, throughout the book.

- A **session** is a single connection to SQL Server, identified by a unique `SessionID` value. It is initiated through an application when the *open* method is used on a *connection* object or through a tool like SSMS when the **File | Connect** menu item is selected. Even though multiple sessions may originate from the same application (and many query windows opened by the same user using the same SSMS instance), as far as SQL Server is concerned, these are all completely separate SQL Server sessions.

- **Locking** occurs when a SQL Server session takes "ownership" of a resource by acquiring a lock, prior to performing a particular action on that resource, such as reading or updating. Locking will stay in effect until SQL Server releases the locks. Note that locking itself is not a problem; it has very little measurable impact on any aspect of our systems, including performance, except when it results in blocking or deadlocking, or when we are performing excessive monitoring of our system locks.

- **Blocking** occurs when at least two sessions desire concurrent access to the same resource. One session acquires a lock on the resource, in order to perform some action, and so renders that resource temporarily unavailable to other sessions. As a result, other sessions requiring the same resource are temporarily blocked. Typically, the blocked sessions will gain control of the resource after the blocking session releases the locks, so that access to the resource is serialized. Note that not all concurrent access will cause blocking; it is dependent on the operations being performed by the sessions, which determines the type of locks that are acquired.

- **A deadlock** occurs when two sessions mutually block each other. Neither one can release the resources it holds until it acquires a lock on the resource the other session holds. A deadlock can also involve more than two sessions, trapped in a circular chain of dependencies. For example, session A may hold a resource that session B wants, and in turn session A is waiting for session C to release a resource. Session B may also hold a resource that session C wants. So session A is blocking B and is blocked by C, session B is blocking C and is blocked by A, and session C is blocking A and is blocked by B. None of the three sessions can proceed.

- **Pressure** is a term used to indicate a state where competition for access to a certain resource is causing performance issues. In a database with well-designed tables and queries, SQL Server acquires and releases locks quickly and any blocking is fleeting, and undetectable by the end-user. However, in certain circumstances, such as when long-running transactions hold locks on a resource for a long time, or where a very high number of sessions all require access to the same shared resource, blocking issues can escalate to the point where one session that is blocked, in turn blocks other sessions, which in turn block others. As the "queue" of blocked sessions grows longer, so the load on the system increases and more and more users start to experience unacceptable delays. In such cases, then we say that the resource is experiencing pressure.

The Hands-On Exercises

This book will provide the reader with scripts for hands-on exercises, shown as listings, to explore locking details and multi-user behavior. The exercises will also illustrate some of the methods for troubleshooting problems with blocking, deadlocking and other types of conflicts. You can download these scripts from the following URL: WWW.SIMPLE-TALK.COM/REDGATEBOOKS/KALENDELANEY/SQLSERVERCONCURRENCY_ CODE.ZIP.

Most of my examples will be based on the readily available `AdventureWorks` database, which you can download from Microsoft's codeplex site at: HTTP://MSFTDBPRODSAMPLES.CODEPLEX.COM/RELEASES/VIEW/4004.

You can run the file **AdventureWorksDB.msi** to copy the data and log files to your hard drive and then, using SQL Server Management Studio, you can attach the files to create the `AdventureWorks` database on your preferred SQL Server instance. When necessary, I will provide scripts to create slightly larger tables, or new tables with particular properties that can demonstrate a behavior under discussion. I will be able to explain, and you will be able to experience, the concurrency behavior issues by establishing multiple connections through SSMS's query windows.

Chapter 1: Concurrency and Transactions

When using either the pessimistic or optimistic concurrency model, a conflict can occur if multiple sessions are "competing" to modify the same data at the same time. In such situations, several resource contention and data integrity issues can arise, such as:

- **Preventable read phenomena** – The ANSI (American National Standards Institute) SQL Standard defines three phenomena (dirty reads, non-repeatable reads and phantom reads), which can be allowed or prevented, depending on the ANSI-standard transaction isolation level in use: READ UNCOMMITTED, READ COMMITTED (the default), REPEATABLE READ, or SERIALIZABLE

- **Lost updates** – One session accidentally overwrites modifications performed by another

- **Excessive blocking** – A "queue" of blocked processes forms, causing pressure on the resource and unacceptable delays to end-users

- **Deadlocks** – Mutual blocking between sessions such that further progress is impossible. SQL Server will choose one of the deadlocked sessions as the "victim," roll it back, and issue a 1205 error message to the affected client.

In this chapter, we'll review and demonstrate the four standard transaction isolation levels and the associated read phenomena, which are dirty reads, non-repeatable reads, and phantom reads.

We'll also consider the each of the concurrency models, pessimistic and optimistic, and discuss, anecdotally, how we might use either technique to prevent lost updates. The pessimistic approach uses locks to block subsequent sessions from modifying a resource until the current session has completed its work. In the optimistic approach, we raise and handle an error, should conflict occur.

There will be a detailed discussion of resource contention issues, namely blocking and deadlocks, in Chapter 5. However, it's worth noting here that if your solution to preventing read phenomena is to use a more restrictive isolation level, or you adopt a pessimistic approach to preventing lost updates, then you increase the risk that your databases will suffer from these contention issues.

Pessimistic Versus Optimistic Concurrency

The degree to which any given instance of SQL Server can support concurrent data access depends on the concurrency model used by SQL Server and, to some extent, on the application logic employed by the programmer.

By default, SQL Server adopts a **pessimistic** approach to concurrency; it assumes that enough concurrent data modification operations are in the system such that problems will occur, and will lead to data integrity issues unless it takes measures to prevent them. Pessimistic concurrency avoids conflicts by acquiring locks while reading data, so no other sessions can modify that data. It also acquires locks while modifying data, so no other sessions can access that data for either reading or modifying. In other words, in a pessimistic concurrency environment, readers block writers and writers block readers.

SQL Server mediates potential problems between competing transactions by implementing a specified transaction isolation level (see the later section on *Transaction isolation levels* for full details). Each of the three commonly used ANSI-standard isolation levels (READ COMMITTED, REPEATABLE READ and SERIALIZABLE) is implemented by SQL Server in a pessimistic fashion, in that locks are acquired to prevent problems. For example, under the READ COMMITTED transaction isolation level (the default level), SQL Server will acquire shared and exclusive locks to prevent "interference" between concurrent transactions. When one of the more restrictive, standard isolation levels is used (REPEATABLE READ or SERIALIZABLE), SQL Server will acquire and hold locks for longer durations, in order to further minimize or eliminate the degree of possible interference. The downside here, of course, is that sessions hold locks for longer durations, so there will be an accompanying reduction in concurrency as lock-holding sessions block more and more lock-requesting sessions from accessing their required data. We'll see all the details of pessimistic concurrency, including information about the duration of locks in the various standard isolation levels, in Chapters 2–5.

Optimistic concurrency, by contrast, assumes that there are sufficiently few conflicting data modification operations in the system that any single transaction is unlikely to modify data that another transaction is modifying. The default behavior of optimistic concurrency is to use a technology called row versioning, available in SQL Server via one of the relatively new snapshot-based isolation levels, introduced in SQL Server 2005. When using one of the snapshot-based isolation levels, SQL Server maintains a time-stamped version store in the `tempdb` database, containing all the previously committed versions of any data rows since the beginning of the oldest open transaction.

If a transaction encounters an exclusive lock on data it needs to read, rather than wait till the lock is released it simply retrieves, from the version store, the version of the rows consistent with either when the current statement (`READ_COMMITTED_SNAPSHOT` mode) or transaction (`SNAPSHOT` mode) started. Under the snapshot-based isolation levels, `SELECT` operations do not acquire shared locks; instead, they simply read the required row versions, consistent with the time the query or transaction started, from the version store, and thus do not block modification operations.

Writers can and will block writers, however, and this is what can cause conflicts. We'll discuss the snapshot-based isolation levels in more detail in Chapter 6.

Transactions

Regardless of which concurrency model is in use, pessimistic or optimistic, we need to understand transaction management and isolation levels. On any multi-user system, the topics of transaction management and concurrency are closely related, and before we discuss the details of SQL Server's concurrency management, we need to briefly review the various methods that SQL Server can use to manage transactions, and the options that a developer has for changing how transactions are managed.

Transaction properties

The simplest definition of a transaction is that it is a single unit of work; a task or set of tasks that together form an "all-or-nothing" operation. If some event interrupts a transaction in the middle, so that not *all* of it was completed, the system should treat the transaction as if it never occurred at all. Transactions can apply to other kinds of systems besides databases, but since this is a database-specific book, we'll be concerned only with database transactions. A transaction can be short, like changing the price of one book in the inventory, or long, like updating the quantity sold of every inventory item at the beginning of an accounting period.

Transactions have four basic properties, called the ACID properties, which guarantee the validity of the data after the completion of any transaction.

- **Atomicity** – A transaction is treated as a single unit of work. Either it completes entirely, or the system has no "memory" of it happening at all. This applies to transactions of any size, whether two rows are being inserted, or 10 million rows are being updated.

- **Consistency** – A transaction will leave data in a meaningful state when it completes. In a relational database, all constraints will be applied to the transaction's modifications to maintain data integrity. Internal data structures, such as the trees and linked lists used for maintaining indexes, will be correct at the end of a transaction. A transaction cannot leave data in a state that violates uniqueness or referential integrity.

- **Isolation** – The changes that one transaction makes should not interfere with the changes that another transaction makes; each transaction should be executed as if it were the only work that the database system was performing.

- **Durability** – Once a transaction completes, its effects are permanent and recoverable. If the system shuts down, either intentionally or because of a system crash, any time after a transaction was completed (or committed) then, when the system starts again, the changes made by completed transactions are available.

SQL Server can guarantee the ACID properties because of the way it acquires and manages locks. However, by default, SQL Server guarantees only three out of the four: atomicity, consistency and durability. If we need SQL Server to guarantee isolation, we'll need to request a higher isolation level than the default (discussed further in Chapter 2).

Transaction scope

SQL Server supports several different ways to define the beginning and end of a transaction. Two methods are available by default, and two are only available under specific conditions.

The default types of transactions are **auto-commit** transactions and **explicit** transactions.

An **auto-commit** transaction is any single data modification operation. In other words, any `INSERT`, `UPDATE` or `DELETE` statement (as well as others, such as `MERGE` and `BULK INSERT`), by itself, is automatically a transaction. If we modify one row, or one million rows, in a single `UPDATE` statement, SQL Server will consider the `UPDATE` operation to be an atomic operation, and will modify either all the rows or none of the rows. If there is a server failure in the middle of the modification operation then, when SQL Server recovers, it will be as if no modifications ever happened. With an auto-commit transaction, there is no way to force a rollback, manually. A transaction rollback will only occur when there is a system failure.

An **explicit** transaction uses the `BEGIN TRANSACTION` (or `BEGIN TRAN`) statement to indicate the beginning of the transaction, and either a `COMMIT TRANSACTION` or a `ROLLBACK TRANSACTION` statement to indicate the end. In between, the transaction can include any number of statements.

Typically, our code will include some sort of test to determine whether the transaction should be committed or rolled back. Since the book's intent is not to provide a complete treatise on transaction management, we won't go into further details here. In the context of locking and blocking, we only need to know *when* a transaction is considered finished.

The non-default types of transactions are **implicit** transactions and **batch-scoped** transactions.

For **implicit** transactions, a session must be in implicit transaction mode, invoked with a SET option: SET IMPLICIT_TRANSACTIONS ON. In implicit transaction mode, the start of any transaction is implied. In other words, any data manipulation language (DML) statement (such as INSERT, UPDATE, DELETE and even SELECT) will automatically start a transaction. In addition, quite a few other statements will start a transaction; check SQL Server's Books Online, at HTTP://MSDN.MICROSOFT.COM/EN-US/LIBRARY/MSI87807.ASPX, for the complete list. Although, in this mode, the start of the transaction is implied, the end of the transaction must be explicit, and the transaction is not finished until we issue either a ROLLBACK TRAN or COMMIT TRAN. This mode is mainly for use by developers who have come to SQL Server from other database management systems, such as Oracle or DB2, which deal with transactions in a different way. However, I strongly recommend that you get used to working with SQL Server's default transaction management options because all the documentation and all books and magazine articles about SQL Server assume you are using that mode. If you must use implicit transaction mode for compatibility with other systems or applications, you'll probably be better off not mixing and matching the two modes, but rather having all your sessions and all your transactions using implicit transaction mode.

Introduced in SQL Server 2005, we invoke **batch-scoped** transactions by requesting the option **Multiple Active Result Sets** (or MARS) in the client connection string. In those connections, SQL Server will roll back any batch that includes a BEGIN TRAN but does not include a COMMIT TRAN. The purpose of MARS is to avoid a problem called "application deadlock," which we'll discuss in Chapter 4, in the section on sharing locks across connections.

Transaction isolation

Every transaction runs in one particular transaction isolation level, which determines how sensitive your application is to changes made by other users' transactions, and how long SQL Server must hold locks to protect against these changes. The ANSI SQL standard defines four levels of isolation for transactions. SQL Server supports all four of these levels, listed in order of increasing restrictiveness, in terms of the **read phenomena** permitted:

- **READ UNCOMMITTED** – allows dirty reads, non-repeatable reads and phantom reads

- **READ COMMITTED** – prevents dirty reads, allows non-repeatable reads and phantom reads

- **REPEATABLE READ** – prevents dirty reads and non-repeatable reads but a llows phantom reads

- **SERIALIZABLE** – prevents all read phenomena.

With the exception of READ UNCOMMITTED, each of these isolations levels is pessimistic in nature. In other words, when transactions are operating in one of these modes, SQL Server will acquire shared and exclusive locks in order to prevent data being read that is currently being modified by another transaction, and to prevent other transactions modifying data that is currently being read. In addition, SQL Server 2005 (and later) offers a new optimistic isolation level, called SNAPSHOT isolation, plus an optimistic alternative to READ COMMITTED isolation (READ_COMMITTED_SNAPSHOT), both of which can ensure consistent results without the need to acquire shared locks, and so can enhance concurrency. We'll discuss the snapshot-based isolation levels in more detail in Chapter 6.

Controlling the isolation level

SQL Server's default isolation level is **READ COMMITTED**, but an application can override this setting by using the following **SET** command:

```
SET TRANSACTION ISOLATION LEVEL
    [READ UNCOMMITTED | READ COMMITTED | REPEATABLE
    READ | SNAPSHOT | SERIALIZABLE]
```

The **SET** command will control the isolation level for all queries submitted over the current connection, until the isolation level is changed, or the connection is terminated. In other words, every time an application makes a new connection (or we open a new query editor window in SSMS), it starts a new session in the SQL Server instance, and any transactions within that new session will use the **READ COMMITTED** isolation level, by default.

You may be wondering if there is a way to change SQL Server's isolation level server-wide, so that, by default, every connection uses an isolation level other than **READ COMMITTED**. The answer is no; the isolation level must be set at the connection level, or within a query. We can control the isolation level for individual queries by using **Lock Hints**, covered later in the book, in Chapter 4.

Preventable read phenomena

The easiest way to define the differences between the various ANSI isolation levels is to describe the set of behaviors that are either permitted or forbidden, depending on which isolation level is in use. The three behaviors, also called "preventable read phenomena," are:

- Dirty reads
- Non-repeatable reads
- Phantom reads.

Dirty reads

This behavior occurs when a transaction reads uncommitted data. If one transaction has changed data but not committed the change, and another transaction is allowed to read that changed data, then there is a strong possibility that the data will be read in an inconsistent state.

For example, consider a stock management application for a factory that receives and distributes SuperWidgets. A number of sales clerks log deliveries and shipments, updating the SuperWidgets inventory item, as appropriate.

Currently, there are only 25 widgets in the stock inventory database, but a new shipment of 50 widgets is just in, so Clerk A starts a transaction and issues an **UPDATE** to reflect a new stock level of 75. At that point, a Clerk B receives an order for 60 widgets and checks the inventory. If Clerk B's transaction permits dirty reads, Clerk B would see 75 widgets and so could authorize the sale, for next-day delivery to a customer. Meanwhile, just as Clerk A prepares to confirm the stock update transaction, he receives a message that a fault has been detected with the batch of widgets, and that they need to be returned to the manufacturer. As a result, he cancels (rolls back) the transaction; Clerk A has authorized an order that the company cannot fulfill, due to insufficient stock.

By default, SQL Server does not allow dirty reads. Keep in mind that the transaction updating the data has no control over whether or not another transaction can read its data before it's committed. The decision regarding whether or not to read "dirty" data lies entirely in the hands of the reading transaction.

Non-repeatable reads

This behavior is also called **inconsistent analysis**. A read is non-repeatable if a query might get different values when reading the same data in two separate reads within the same transaction. This can happen when a separate transaction updates the same data, after the first read but before the second read.

In the receiving room example, suppose that a manager comes in to do a spot check of the current inventory. She walks up to each clerk, asking the total number of widgets received that day, and adding the numbers on her calculator. When she's done, she wants to double-check the result, so she goes back to the first clerk. However, if Clerk A received more widgets between the manager's first and second inquiries, the total will be different each time and the reads are non-repeatable.

Phantom reads

This behavior occurs when membership in a set changes. It can happen only when a query with a predicate, such as WHERE count_of_widgets < 10, is involved. A phantom occurs if two SELECT operations using the same predicate in the same transaction return a different number of rows. For example, let's say that our manager is still doing spot checks of inventory. This time, she goes around the receiving room and notes which clerks have fewer than ten widgets. After she completes the list, she goes back around to offer advice to everyone with a low total. However, imagine that during her first walk-through the manager failed to include in her list a clerk who had just returned from a break, and had fewer than ten widgets. This additional clerk (or row) is a phantom.

Transaction isolation levels

We can allow or prevent these read phenomena by adjusting the transaction isolation level within the SQL Server connection. Remember that the default isolation level, if none is specified, is READ COMMITTED.

Table 1-1 summarizes which of the potentially undesirable behaviors are possible at each isolation level, and whether the isolation level uses pessimistic or optimistic concurrency. The ANSI SQL Committee has defined four isolation levels for the SQL language. Microsoft SQL Server supports all four, and added a fifth, SNAPSHOT isolation, in SQL Server 2005.

Transaction Isolation Level	Behaviors Allowed			Concurrency Model
	Dirty Read	Non-repeatable Read	Phantoms	
READ UNCOMMITTED	Yes	Yes	Yes	Pessimistic
READ COMMITTED	No	Yes	Yes	Pessimistic
(default for SQL Server)	No	Yes	Yes	Optimistic
REPEATABLE READ	No	No	Yes	Pessimistic
SNAPSHOT	No	No	No	Optimistic
SERIALIZABLE	No	No	No	Pessimistic

Table 1-1: Which isolation levels permit which behaviors?

Note that, in SQL Server 2005 and later, there is both a pessimistic and an optimistic implementation of the default isolation level, READ COMMITTED. By default, transactions against a SQL Server database will use the pessimistic form of READ COMMITTED isolation, acquiring locks to prevent the read phenomena discussed previously. However, if we enable the READ_COMMITTED_SNAPSHOT option for that database then, by default, transactions will use the optimistic form of READ COMMITTED isolation, preventing read phenomena without the need for locking, via use of the tempdb version store. The difference between the two variations of READ_COMMITTED will become clearer after we discuss how SQL Server controls each of these concurrency models.

To see the behavior in each ANSI isolation level, we'll look at some example code. First, create a table called IsolationTest in a database called IsolationDB and populate the table with a few rows, by running the code in Listing 1-1. I'll refer to the IsolationTest table in examples for each of the four ANSI isolation levels. The fifth isolation level, SNAPSHOT, will be covered in Chapter 6, where we discuss the details of optimistic concurrency.

Unless stated otherwise, you can run all the code using a Query Window in
SQL Server Management Studio.

```
-- Create a database and table for testing the isolation levels
USE master
GO
IF EXISTS ( SELECT   1
            FROM     sys.databases
            WHERE    name = 'IsolationDB' )
    DROP DATABASE IsolationDB ;
GO
CREATE DATABASE IsolationDB ;
GO
USE IsolationDB ;
GO
CREATE TABLE IsolationTest
    (
        col1 INT PRIMARY KEY ,
        col2 VARCHAR(20)
    ) ;
GO
INSERT  INTO IsolationTest
VALUES  ( 10, 'The first row' ) ;
INSERT  INTO IsolationTest
VALUES  ( 20, 'The second row' ) ;
INSERT  INTO IsolationTest
VALUES  ( 30, 'The third row' ) ;
INSERT  INTO IsolationTest
VALUES  ( 40, 'The fourth row' ) ;
INSERT  INTO IsolationTest
VALUES  ( 50, 'The fifth row' ) ;
GO
```

Listing 1-1:   Create a database and table for running the isolation level exercises.

READ UNCOMMITTED

READ UNCOMMITTED isolation level allows a transaction to read any data currently on a data or index page, regardless of whether or not the transaction that wrote that data has been committed. For example, although another user might have a transaction in progress that performs data modifications, and that transaction is holding exclusive locks on the data, a transaction using the READ UNCOMMITTED isolation level can read the data anyway (a dirty read), and possibly take further actions based on the values read.

The potential problem with dirty reads is that the user who started the modification transaction might then decide to roll it back so, logically, those changes *never occurred*. If we act based on a data value that essentially *never existed*, then that decision or action might not be valid.

Let's see how the READ UNCOMMITTED isolation level behaves. In Listing 1-2, run Step 1 to begin a transaction (without committing it) and then open a new query window to run Step 2. Use the IsolationDB database for each connection.

```
-- Step 1:
-- Start a transaction but don't commit it
USE IsolationDB ;
GO
BEGIN TRAN
UPDATE   IsolationTest
SET      col2 = 'New Value' ;
--<EXECUTE>

-- Step 2:
-- Start a new connection and change your isolation level
USE IsolationDB ;
GO
SET TRANSACTION ISOLATION LEVEL READ UNCOMMITTED ;
SELECT   *
FROM     IsolationTest ;
--<EXECUTE>
```

```
-- Step 3:
-- Return to the connection from Step 1 and issue a ROLLBACK
ROLLBACK TRANSACTION ;
--<EXECUTE>

-- Step 4:
-- Rerun the SELECT statement in the connection from Step 2
SELECT  *
FROM    IsolationTest ;
-- <EXECUTE>
```

Listing 1-2:   Hands-on exercise – READ UNCOMMITTED isolation level.

In the results returned from the query in Step 2, notice that all the values in col2 are the string 'New Value', even though the transaction in the first connection has not yet committed. In fact, the transaction might never commit. If we take some action, based on an understanding that all the values are the same, we could regret it if the changes turned out not to be permanent. Back in the first connection, roll back the transaction, as shown in Step 3.

For Step 4, rerun the SELECT statement in the second connection to see that all the values in col2 have reverted to their original values. If you're following along with these examples, make sure you close all your connections before proceeding, so that we're sure that SQL Server will release any outstanding locks.

The potential for reading dirty is far from the only problem that can arise when using READ UNCOMMITTED isolation level. If a query running under READ UNCOMMITTED isolation level performs a scan of a table (or is scanning a range of data within a table), it is possible that a separate transaction could update a row of data, causing that row to move to a new location. If the scan started before the update and read the initial version of the row, the row might move to a page not yet read, and the query could end up reading it again, later on in the same scan. Therefore, the query would read the same data multiple times.

Alternatively, a row that has not yet been read might be updated, and moved to a page in the table already read, so that the scan would never read the row at all, and completely miss some data.

For these reasons, I r strongly ecommend that you don't make extensive use of **READ UNCOMMITTED** isolation level within application code. This includes using the **NOLOCK** hint, which invokes **READ UNCOMMITTED** for a single table in a single query. We'll look at hints in more detail in Chapter 4.

READ COMMITTED

READ COMMITTED is SQL Server's default isolation level. It ensures that an operation will never read data another transaction has changed but not committed. However, because SQL Server holds locks for **SELECT** operations for only a short time, if a transaction running with **READ COMMITTED** isolation re-reads data, that data might have changed, or new rows might appear that meet the criteria of the original query.

So **READ COMMITTED** behavior has two aspects. Firstly, it prevents dirty reads but, secondly, it still allows non-repeatable reads and phantom reads.

To see the first aspect, we can simply repeat the previous example, but with the second connection using the default **READ COMMITTED** isolation level, rather than **READ UNCOMMITTED**, as shown by Steps 1 through 4, in Listing 1-3. The second connection blocks on its **SELECT** statement; it can't read the changes the first connection has made but not yet committed (or rolled back). Once we roll back the transaction, in Step 3, the query in Step 2 completes and returns the original data.

```
-- Step 1:
-- Start a transaction but don't commit it
USE IsolationDB ;
GO
BEGIN TRAN
UPDATE  IsolationTest
SET     col2 = 'New Value' ;
--<EXECUTE>

-- Step 2:
-- Start a new connection and change your isolation level
USE IsolationDB ;
GO
SET TRANSACTION ISOLATION LEVEL READ COMMITTED ;
SELECT  *
FROM    IsolationTest ;
--<EXECUTE>
-- You should notice that the process blocks, and returns
-- no data or messages!

-- To finish up, perform the following two steps:
-- Step 3:
-- Return to the connection from Step 1 and issue a ROLLBACK
ROLLBACK TRANSACTION ;
--<EXECUTE>

-- Step 4:
-- Rerun the SELECT statement in the connection from Step 2
SELECT  *
FROM    IsolationTest ;
-- <EXECUTE>
-- Verify that the data is available
```

Listing 1-3: A SELECT statement blocking with READ COMMITTED isolation level.

To see the second aspect of READ COMMITTED behavior (specifically, non-repeatable reads), close all the connections from the previous example, and open two new connections, using IsolationDB again. Listing 1-4 shows the code. In the first connection, Step 1 will make sure the isolation level is the default READ COMMITTED, and then it will start a transaction that reads data from the IsolationTest table to compute an average.

In the second connection, Step 2 will **UPDATE** the table. Assuming that the query in Step 1 has finished processing, the **UPDATE** will succeed, even though the first connection is still inside a transaction. Note that the **UPDATE** is an auto-commit transaction and so SQL Server will commit the **UPDATE** and release the locks as soon as it completes.

In Step 3, return to the first connection and run the same **SELECT** statement. The average value is now different and we have a non-repeatable read. The default **READ COMMITTED** isolation level prevents other connections from reading data being modified, but only prevents other connections from changing data being read, while the read operation is in progress. Once it is complete, other transactions can change the data, even if the reading transaction is still open. As a result, there is no guarantee that we'll see the same data if we rerun the **SELECT** within the transaction.

```
-- Step 1:
-- Read data in the default isolation level
USE IsolationDB
SET TRANSACTION ISOLATION LEVEL READ COMMITTED ;
BEGIN TRAN
SELECT  AVG(col1)
FROM    IsolationTest ;
--<EXECUTE>

-- Step 2:
-- In a new  connection, update the table:
USE IsolationDB ;
UPDATE  IsolationTest
SET     col1 = 500
WHERE   col1 = 50 ;
--<EXECUTE>

-- Step 3:
-- Go back to the first connection and
--   run the same SELECT statement:
SELECT  AVG(col1)
FROM    IsolationTest ;
--<EXECUTE>
```

Listing 1-4:   READ COMMITTED isolation level allows data to be changed by other connections.

The isolation level READ COMMITTED guarantees only that a transaction will not read uncommitted data. However, the ANSI SQL specification does not specify any particular mechanism that a database system should use to implement READ COMMITTED isolation, and so prevent dirty reads.

As of SQL Server 2005, SQL Server provides two different ways of preventing a transaction from reading dirty data in the READ COMMITTED isolation level. The default method we have just seen, using pessimistic concurrency, locks the data modified inside a transaction, and the locks keep other processes from accessing that data. It also takes shared locks for short periods to prevent data being modified while it is being read.

In SQL Server 2005, the alternative form of READ COMMITTED, called READ_ COMMITTED_SNAPSHOT, uses optimistic concurrency. As one would expect, its behavior is the same as the default in terms of the read phenomena, i.e. it prevents dirty reads, but allows non-repeatable reads and phantom reads. However, this optimistic implementation of the READ COMMITTED level prevents dirty reads, *without* blocking other transactions.

There is a whole chapter on optimistic concurrency later in the book, but let's see a quick example of how SQL Server can use this completely different method to enforce READ COMMITTED isolation.

The only change we need to make is at the database level, turning on the READ_ COMMITTED_SNAPSHOT database option. Other than that, listing 1-5 is the same script as Listing 1-3.

```
-- Step 1:
-- First close all other connections to make sure no one is using
--   the IsolationDB datatabase

-- Step 2:
--   Change the database option to enable "read committed snapshot"
ALTER DATABASE IsolationDB SET READ_COMMITTED_SNAPSHOT ON ;
--<EXECUTE>
```

```
-- Step 3:
-- Start a transaction but don't commit it
USE IsolationDB ;
GO
BEGIN TRAN
UPDATE  IsolationTest
SET     col2 = 'New Value' ;
--<EXECUTE>


-- Step 4:
-- Start a new connection and change your isolation level
USE IsolationDB ;
GO
SET TRANSACTION ISOLATION LEVEL READ COMMITTED ;
SELECT  *
FROM    IsolationTest ;
--<EXECUTE>
-- You should notice that the second connection is not blocked, but
-- it does not return the changed data. The results you get are the
-- original committed data, before the UPDATE in Step 3 was performed
-- no data or messages!

-- To finish up, perform the following steps:
-- Step 5:
-- Return to the connection from Step 1 and issue a ROLLBACK
ROLLBACK TRANSACTION ;
--<EXECUTE>


-- Step 6:
-- Now close all other connections to make sure no one is using
-- the IsolationDB datatabase

-- Step 7:
--  Change the database option to disable "read committed snapshot"
ALTER DATABASE IsolationDB SET READ_COMMITTED_SNAPSHOT OFF ;
--<EXECUTE>
```

Listing 1-5:   The SELECT statement doesn't block when the database is using
READ COMMITTED SNAPSHOT isolation or RCSI.

Chapter 6, *Optimistic Concurrency*, will explain exactly how we are able to see the previous
values of the data without any blocking.

REPEATABLE READ

The **REPEATABLE READ** isolation level adds to the properties of **READ COMMITTED** by ensuring that if a transaction re-reads data, or if a query is reissued within the same transaction, then the same data will be returned. In other words, issuing the same query twice within a transaction won't pick up any changes to data values that were made by another transaction. A second transaction cannot modify the data that a first transaction has read, as long as that first transaction has not yet committed or rolled back.

To see **REPEATABLE READ** behavior, close all the connections to the `IsolationDB` database, and open two new ones. Steps 1 through 3 in Listing 1-6 will issue the same two queries as in Listing 1-4, but this time, the first connection will set the isolation level to **REPEATABLE READ** in Step 1.

In Step 2, the second connection will have to use a slightly different **UPDATE** statement, because the value of 50 for `col1` no longer exists. This **UPDATE** will block when it tries to modify the `IsolationTest` table. In Step 3, the first connection will get the same result when it reissues its original **SELECT**.

```
-- Step 1:
-- Read data in the Repeatable Read isolation level
USE IsolationDB ;
SET TRANSACTION ISOLATION LEVEL REPEATABLE READ ;
BEGIN TRAN
SELECT  AVG(col1)
FROM    IsolationTest ;
--<EXECUTE>

-- Step 2:
-- In the second connection, update the table:
USE IsolationDB ;
UPDATE  IsolationTest
SET     col1 = 5000
WHERE   col1 = 500 ;
--<EXECUTE>
-- You should notice that the UPDATE process blocks,
-- and returns no data or messages
```

```
-- Step 3:
-- Go back to the first connection and
-- run the same SELECT statement:
SELECT  AVG(col1)
FROM    IsolationTest ;
--<EXECUTE>
```

Listing 1-6:   REPEATABLE READ isolation level doesn't allow another process to update values the first one has read.

Preventing non-repeatable reads, or allowing the first connection to make sure it will reread the same data, is a desirable safeguard, but it comes at a price. The cost of this extra safeguard is that SQL Server holds all the shared locks in a transaction until the completion (**COMMIT** or **ROLLBACK**) of the transaction.

However, **REPEATABLE READ** isolation doesn't prevent all possible read phenomena. It protects only the data that has already been read. Listing 1-7 demonstrates what this protection means. Close all connections, and open two new ones connecting to IsolationDB. In the first connection, start a transaction in **REPEATABLE READ** isolation level and look for all rows that meet a certain condition, as shown in Step 4.

In the second connection, Step 5 will insert a new row. Now go back to the first connection, and re-execute the **SELECT** in Step 6.

```
-- Close all connections and open two new ones

-- Step 4:
USE IsolationDB ;
SET TRANSACTION ISOLATION LEVEL REPEATABLE READ
BEGIN TRAN
SELECT  *
FROM    IsolationTest
WHERE   col1 BETWEEN 20 AND 40
--<EXECUTE>
```

35

```
-- Step 5:
-- In the second connection, insert new data
USE IsolationDB ;
INSERT  INTO IsolationTest
VALUES  ( 25, 'New Row' ) ;
--<EXECUTE>

-- Step 6:
-- Go back to the first connection and rerun the SELECT
SELECT  *
FROM    IsolationTest
WHERE   col1 BETWEEN 20 AND 40 ;
--<EXECUTE>-- Notice one additional row
```

Listing 1-7:   REPEATABLE READ isolation level does allow new rows to be inserted
                that satisfy the query condition.

Upon the second execution of the same SELECT statement, the new row appears, called
a **phantom**. The row didn't even exist the first time we ran the SELECT statement, so it
wasn't locked. We can prevent phantoms with the SERIALIZABLE isolation level.

SERIALIZABLE

The SERIALIZABLE isolation level ensures that, if a query is reissued, no data will have
changed and no new rows will appear. In other words, we won't see phantoms if the same
query is issued twice within a transaction. In Listing 1-8, we rerun the example from
Listing 1-7, inserting a row with a col1 value of 35, but this time setting the isolation level
to SERIALIZABLE in the first connection. The second connection will block when we try
to do the INSERT, and the first connection will read exactly the same rows each time.

```
-- Open two new connections

-- Step 1:
-- In the first connection, start a transaction
USE IsolationDB ;
SET TRANSACTION ISOLATION LEVEL SERIALIZABLE ;
BEGIN TRAN
SELECT  *
FROM    IsolationTest
WHERE   col1 BETWEEN 20 AND 40 ;
--<EXECUTE>

-- Step 2:
-- In the second connection, insert new data
USE IsolationDB
INSERT  INTO IsolationTest
VALUES  ( 35, 'Another New Row' ) ;
-- Notice that the INSERT will block
--<EXECUTE>


-- Step 3:
-- Go back to the first connection and rerun the SELECT
SELECT  *
FROM    IsolationTest
WHERE   col1 BETWEEN 20 AND 40 ;
--<EXECUTE>
-- Notice no new rows
```

Listing 1-8: SERIALIZABLE isolation level does not allow insertion of a new row.

Again, we pay a price to prevent phantoms. In addition to locking all the data has been read, enforcing the SERIALIZABLE isolation level, and so preventing phantoms, requires that SQL Server also lock data that doesn't exist (see the *Key-range Locks* section in Chapter 3). The SERIALIZABLE level gets its name from the fact that running multiple SERIALIZABLE transactions at the same time is the equivalent of running them one at a time – that is, serially.

SNAPSHOT

There is an entirely new isolation level, introduced in SQL Server 2005 called SNAPSHOT isolation. The only implementation of snapshot isolation uses optimistic concurrency, so we'll save the discussion of this level until the Chapter 6, on optimistic concurrency.

Selecting the right isolation level

Having examined all the ANSI isolation levels, you might want to go back and re-examine Table 1-1.

While preventing blocking, by selecting the READ UNCOMMITTED level, might seem attractive from a concurrency perspective, the price to pay is the prospect of reading incorrect data. At the same time, while preventing all read phenomena, and so guaranteeing more consistent data, is a "good thing," be aware of the tradeoffs in setting your isolation level too high, which is the added cost of acquiring and managing locks, and blocking other processes while those locks are held.

The optimistic isolation levels reduce the amount of blocking, but they do not eliminate it. In addition, they have costs and caveats of their own, which we'll explore in Chapter 6.

The Lost Update Problem

A lost update occurs when the results of one update overwrites the effects of another update, such that it's as if the first update never happened. None of the transaction isolation levels will permit lost updates; in other words, it's impossible for two transactions to update the same data, simultaneously, in such a way that the effect of one of the transactions is lost.

However, as an addendum to this, it's worth noting that transaction isolation levels *only* prevent conflict between transactions that overlap in time. There are circumstances, usually involving data querying for subsequent updates, via an end-user form, where transactions don't overlap in time, from the database's perspective, and so, from the end-users perspective, the effects of one transaction can be overwritten by another and so are "lost."

Consider the situation below, which is a classic example of the lost update problem.

> *Clerks at locations all over the city operate a ticket-selling application. Customer1 at Location1 asks to see all the available seats for Friday night's big show, and so Clerk1 reads the relevant data into the booking form. While Customer1 is debating the pros and cons of taking seat 1A or 1Z, Customer2, at Location2, also asks to see the available seats for Friday and so Clerk2 reads in the same data. Until Customer1 confirms a choice, both Seats 1A and 1Z appear as available to Customer2; she makes a quick choice and Clerk2 issues the appropriate update, selling Seat 1A toCustomer2. However, Clerk1's form, if concurrency is poorly managed, may still reflect that Seat 1A is available, and so Clerk1 could issue a subsequent update, selling Seat 1A to Customer1. In effect, Clerk2's update has been lost and Customer1 will own Seat 1A, but both customers will turn up at the event expecting to sit there.*

There are many variations on this recipe for lost updates, with the central ingredient being that an application first reads data and then, at some later point, updates it. Generally, lost updates will only occur in a system that does not manage concurrency properly, and it can be considered an application bug. In our example, it's clear that the application needs to check that the data has not changed between querying it and updating it.

We can avoid lost updates in SQL Server using either a pessimistic or an optimistic approach to concurrency. The difference between these two concurrency models lies in whether update conflicts can be avoided *before* they occur, or can be dealt with in some manner *as* they occur. We'll provide here only a high-level overview of the two different approaches, and discuss, anecdotally, how each might prevent lost updates.

Pessimistic concurrency avoids conflicts by acquiring locks on data that is being read, so no other processes can modify that data. It also acquires locks on data being modified, so no other processes can access that data for either reading or modifying. In other words, readers block writers and writers block readers in a pessimistic concurrency environment. If pessimistic concurrency were implemented correctly in the ticket-selling application, the first clerk or customer to look at the data would cause the data to be locked, and the second clerk or customer could not even see what was available until the first one had made their decision (no matter how long it took.). However, this may require us, as programmers, to "reinforce" SQL Server's pessimistic concurrency model via use, for example, of locking hints (see Chapter 4).

A programmer will need to enforce optimistic concurrency by the use of intelligent programming techniques. For example, when querying data into a form, for subsequent modification, the application logic should store the original values and then check them against the values that exist at the point the modification is issued. If they are different, logic must exist to resolve this conflict and/or handle any error raised. If optimistic concurrency were used in the examples above, when the second clerk or customer tried to run an update, the system would generate an error message that a conflict had been detected and the second update would fail. SQL Server would send an error message to the client application, but it would be up to the application to respond to that error.

Summary

This chapter described what a transaction is and how SQL Server manages your transactions. It also described three behaviors that can occur within transactions that we might want to avoid: dirty reads, non-repeatable reads, and phantoms. Finally, it described the ANSI-standard isolation levels available to applications that allow us to control which of these behaviors we want to allow, and which we want to avoid.

Both pessimistic and optimistic concurrency can encounter problems with excessive blocking. Blocking problems are one of the greatest causes of application performance issues in client/server applications, including web-based applications. Much of the source of the problems is due to the fact that application developers do not understand how SQL Server concurrency management works, and when locking can lead to serious blocking problems. The remainder of this book will remedy that situation by describing the internal details and mechanisms of SQL Server's concurrency management. The next chapter starts the discussion with details of SQL Server's locking mechanisms, and of how SQL Server uses locking to implement the isolation levels, when using the pessimistic concurrency model.

Chapter 2: Locking Basics

Locking is the activity that occurs when a SQL Server session takes "ownership" of a resource prior to performing a particular action on that resource, such as reading or updating it. Keep in mind that locking is just a logical concept, designed to help support the ACID properties of our transactions, so that our data stays consistent. If SQL Server acquired no locks, it could still perform all the actions specified by commands in the SQL language. However, for anyone who cares about data consistency, locks are a good and necessary database mechanism.

However, because locks are a logical concept, not based on physical requirements within the database system, the designers of any relational database system have a lot of flexibility with regard to exactly how to implement locking, and the impact it will have on resource usage within the system.

For the most part, SQL Server makes all locking decisions internally and will usually make the best choices. A good developer or administrator will understand how SQL Server applies and manages locks, but will rarely need to "overrule" SQL Server's choices. Nevertheless, in the rare instances where you may need to exert a measure of control over some aspect of SQL Server locking, there are ways to do that, which we'll discuss in a later chapter.

Locking Overview

Locking is an essential mechanism for allowing multiple users to access and operate on data in a way that avoids inconsistencies in that data. However, it does mean that, when we write SQL code, we must be aware that it's likely that locks will be acquired, in the database, as part of its execution. If we write code in such a way that it forces SQL Server to acquire a very large number of locks, or to hold them for unnecessarily long periods, then this will cause resource contention in the database, other users' transactions will be blocked from accessing the data they need, and the performance of these blocked transactions will be affected.

In the same way, as the ANSI transaction isolation level becomes more restrictive in terms of the permitted read phenomena, so SQL Server will adopt a more "aggressive" locking policy to prevent interference between transactions, and so the likelihood of blocking, and even deadlocking, increases. All of this means that, as database developers and DBAs, we need at least a basic understanding of how locking works in the SQL Server database engine, and how to investigate any blocking-related issues that might arise. In this section, we'll review the following fundamental aspects of this locking mechanism:

- **The unit of data locked (lock resource)** – such as row, page, or table

- **The type of locks acquired (lock mode)** – shared, exclusive, update, and so on

- **The duration of the lock** – how long the lock is held

- **Lock ownership** – the "scope" of the lock (most locks are transaction scoped)

- **Lock metadata** – how to review current locking using the Dynamic Management View (DMV) called `sys.dm_tran_locks`.

Lock resources

SQL Server can lock user data resources at the row, page, or table level. In general, SQL Server will attempt to acquire row-level locks, to allow the highest degree of concurrency. However, as we'll see later, there are conditions that could cause SQL Server to acquire locks on larger units of data either initially, or through a process of "lock escalation."

When SQL Server locks a row in an index, it refers to it, and displays it, as a `KEY` lock, but keep in mind that SQL Server locks the entire index row, not just the key column. In some circumstances, SQL Server can also lock ranges of index rows. Locks on rows in a heap table (one without a clustered index) appear as `RID` (Row ID) locks in the `sys.dm_tran_locks` view.

SQL Server supports two kinds of KEY locks, depending on the isolation level of the current transaction. If the isolation level is READ COMMITTED or REPEATABLE READ, SQL Server attempts to lock the index rows it accesses while processing the query. If the table has a clustered index, then the data rows are at the leaf level of the index, and so row locks for any data in a table with a clustered index will always appear as KEY locks. If the table is a heap, SQL Server might acquire KEY locks for the non-clustered index rows and RID locks for the data rows.

If the isolation level is SERIALIZABLE, we have a special situation, as SQL Server needs to prevent phantom reads. If a query scans a range of data within a transaction, SQL Server needs to lock enough of the table to ensure that another transaction cannot insert a new value into the range being scanned, which would then appear as a phantom if the query was reissued. For this, it employs **key-range locks** (still referred to as KEY locks in the metadata, based on the locked resource).

For example, suppose we have an index on the lastname column in the Employees table. A transaction, shown in Listing 2-1, is running under the SERIALIZABLE isolation level, and reads a range of rows in the Employees table.

```
SET TRANSACTION ISOLATION LEVEL SERIALIZABLE;
BEGIN TRAN
SELECT  *
FROM    Employees
WHERE   LastName BETWEEN 'MacDougal' AND 'McDougall'
```

Listing 2-1:   A transaction performing a range search under SERIALIZABLE isolation.

In addition to disallowing any changes to the data retrieved by this query, SQL Server needs to make sure that no other process can insert a new row for which the LastName value falls in the specified range. For example, no one should be able to insert a row with McDonald, but a row with Mabry would be fine. So here's what SQL Server does: if MacAndrews, MacWorter, and McKenna are sequential leaf-level index key values in the index on LastName, the index rows with MacWorter and McKenna each acquire a key-range lock.

45

A key-range lock implies a locked range of index rows including all values greater than the value of the index key that precedes the locked row, and ends with the locked row.

In this example, we'd have one key-range lock that starts with MacAndrews and ends with MacWorter and another key-range lock that starts with MacWorter and ends with McKenna. These two key-range locks encompass all the values that might satisfy the WHERE clause in the query in Listing 2-1; no transaction could insert data that would fall within this range. To be precise, based on the two values which I've indicated should have a key-range lock, we would say rows that meet either of the two conditions below would not be allowed to be inserted:

```
new_key_value>'MacAndrews' AND new_key_value<= 'MacWorter'
new_key_value>'MacWorter' AND new_key_value<= 'McKenna'
```

These two key-range locks prevent a transaction from inserting MacOwen or McBride, which are in the range that the WHERE clause specifies. However, they also prevent insertion of MacBryde, even though MacBryde is not in the specified range. Key-range locks are not perfect, but they do give much greater concurrency than locking a whole page or the entire table, which were the only possibilities in versions of SQL Server prior to SQL Server 7.

Note that if there is no index on the column specifying the range (in this case, LastName), SQL Server would acquire row or page locks, even in recent versions.

Lock modes

SQL Server uses several types of locks, referred to as **lock modes**. These include shared locks, exclusive locks, and update locks, used to achieve the four required ANSI modes of transaction isolation. The lock mode specifies how restrictive the lock is and what other actions are possible while the lock is held.

Shared locks

By default, SQL Server acquires shared (S) locks automatically when it reads data. A table, page, or individual row of a table or index can hold an S lock. In addition, to support `SERIALIZABLE` transaction isolation, SQL Server can place S locks on a range of index rows. As the name implies, many processes can hold S locks on the same data, but no process can acquire an exclusive lock on data that has an S lock on it (unless the process requesting the exclusive lock is the same process holding the S lock, and no other process has an S lock on the data).

Usually, SQL Server releases S locks as soon as it has finished reading the data. However, use of a higher transaction isolation level, either `REPEATABLE READ` or `SERIALIZABLE`, changes this behavior, so that SQL Server holds S locks until the end of the transaction. In the `sys.dm_tran_locks` view, a `request_mode` of 'S' indicates a shared lock.

Exclusive locks

SQL Server automatically acquires exclusive (X) locks on data in order to modify that data, during an `INSERT`, `UPDATE`, or `DELETE` operation. Only one transaction at a time can hold an X lock on a particular data resource, and X locks remain until the end of the transaction. The changed data is usually unavailable to any other process until the transaction holding the lock either commits or rolls back. However, if a transaction uses the `READ UNCOMMITTED` transaction isolation level, it can read data exclusively locked by another transaction. In the `sys.dm_tran_locks` view, a `request_mode` of 'X' indicates an exclusive lock.

Update locks

Update (U) locks are not really a separate kind of lock, but rather a hybrid of S and X locks. A transaction acquires a U lock when SQL Server executes a data modification operation, but first needs to perform a search to find the resource (for example, the row of data) to modify.

SQL Server doesn't need to place an X lock on the row until it is ready to perform the modification, but it does need to apply some sort of lock as it searches, to protect that same data from modification by another transaction in the time between finding the data and modifying it. Therefore, SQL Server places a U lock on the row, checks the row and, if it meets the criteria, converts it to an X lock.

As SQL Server is searching for the data, it could acquire an S lock on each row it encountered and then determine whether it had found the data it needed. However, there are potential problems with this approach. A situation could occur where two transactions were both searching for the same row to modify (for example, the same customer row in the Customers table), using different access paths, and they could both reach the desired resource at the same time. Each transaction could acquire an S lock on that row, but then each transaction would attempt to convert this lock to an X lock in order to perform the modification, but the S lock held by one transaction prevents the other from doing so. At this point, we have a **deadlock** since neither transaction can proceed (we cover deadlocks in more detail in Chapter 5).

In order or avoid such deadlocks, if a transaction begins a search operation with the intention of eventually modifying data, then SQL Server acquires U locks until it finds the data to modify. U locks are compatible with S locks, but are incompatible with X locks or other U locks. So if two transactions were searching for the same resource, each with the intention of modifying it, then the first one to reach it would acquire a U lock, and then the second one would be blocked until the first was finished. Since the second transaction was blocked, the first is free to convert its U lock to an X lock, make the data modification and release its locks. Then the second transaction could make its change. In the sys.dm_tran_locks view, a request_mode of 'U' indicates an update lock.

Intent locks

Intent locks do not represent a distinct mode of locking. The term "intent" is a qualifier to the modes just discussed. In other words, you can have intent shared (IS) locks, intent exclusive locks (IX), and even intent update locks (IU), indicated in the `request_mode` column of the `sys.dm_tran_locks` view by IS, IX and IU, respectively.

As we've discussed, SQL Server can acquire locks at different levels of granularity (i.e., at the row, page, or table level), and so needs some mechanism that signals whether a component of a resource is already locked. For example, if one transaction attempts to lock a table, SQL Server must be able to determine whether it has already locked a row or a page of that table. Intent locks serve that purpose. Whenever a transaction acquires a lock at a lower level of granularity, it also acquires higher-level intent locks for the same object. For example, a transaction that holds an X lock on a row in the `Customers` table will also hold IX locks on both the page containing that row, and the `Customers` table. These Intent locks will prevent another transaction from locking the entire `Customers` table (acquiring an X lock on the table).

We'll cover in more detail which lock modes are compatible and incompatible in the section on lock compatibility, in Chapter 3.

Lock duration

The length of time that SQL Server holds a lock depends primarily on the mode of the lock and the transaction isolation level that is in effect. READ COMMITTED is SQL Server's default isolation level. At this level, SQL Server releases S locks as soon as it has read and processed the locked data. It holds an X lock until the end of the transaction, whether the transaction is committed or rolled back. It holds a U lock until the end of the transaction, unless it promoted the U lock to an X lock, in which case the X lock, as with all X locks, remains for the duration of the transaction.

If the transaction isolation level is **REPEATABLE READ** or **SERIALIZABLE**, S locks have the same duration as X locks. That is, SQL Server does not release them until the transaction is over.

In addition to changing the transaction isolation level, we can control the lock duration by using lock hints. We'll see details about lock hints in Chapter 4.

Lock ownership

We can think of lock ownership as the *scope* of the lock, and it can affect lock duration. There are three default values for the lock owner, and two additional types of lock ownership that must be explicitly requested. We can observe lock ownership values in the `request_owner_type` column of the **sys.dm_tran_locks** DMV. The default lock owner values are below.

- **TRANSACTION** – Most of the locks discussed in this book are transaction-owned locks. Most of the locks that are involved in blocking and troubleshooting are transaction-owned locks. The duration of transaction-owned locks is as discussed in the previous section.

- **SHARED_TRANSACTION_WORKSPACE** – Every connection in any database (other than `master` or `tempdb`) acquires a lock with this owner by. By observing these locks, SQL Server can tell when a database is in use. **SHARED_TRANSACTION_WORKSPACE** locks are held as long as a connection is using a database.

- **EXCLUSIVE_TRANSACTION_WORKSPACE** – SQL Server acquires a lock with this owner whenever it needs exclusive access to the database. This includes activities such as dropping the database, restoring the database, or changing certain database properties, such as the **READ_ONLY** status. A connection cannot acquire a lock with an owner of **EXCLUSIVE_TRANSACTION_WORKSPACE** if any other connections have a lock owned by a **SHARED_TRANSACTION_WORKSPACE** and, in such cases, SQL Server generates an error message. SQL Server will hold a lock with this owner until the operation needing this lock (dropping, restoring or changing status) is completed.

The purpose of the SHARED_TRANSACTION_WORKSPACE lock owner is to prevent SQL Server from acquiring EXCLUSIVE_TRANSACTION_WORKSPACE locks, that is, to prevent a process from dropping, restoring, or changing readability status for a database, while the database is in use. The reason SQL Server does not acquire these locks for the master and tempdb databases is that these databases cannot be dropped, or have their readability status changed. In addition, we never restore tempdb, and to restore the master database, we must start the entire server in single-user mode so, again, SHARED_TRANSACTION_WORKSPACE locks are unnecessary.

The additional lock owner values are CURSOR and SESSION. We can request the former in a cursor declaration, but we will not discuss this topic further in this book. A SESSION lock is available only through user-defined locks, created with the sp_getapplock stored procedure, as will be discussed in Chapter 4.

Locking metadata

The best source of current lock information is the previously referenced sys.dm_tran_locks DMV. This view replaces the sp_lock procedure, although sp_lock is still available. Although calling a procedure might require less typing than querying the sys.dm_tran_locks view, the latter is much more flexible. Not only are there many more columns of information, providing details about our locks, but as a view, sys.dm_tran_locks can be queried to select just the columns we want, or only the rows that meet our criteria. We can join sys.dm_tran_locks to other views to get aggregate (summary) information on how many locks of each kind SQL Server holds.

Keep in mind that the DMVs are not based on a real table, because the data they expose isn't really stored in a SQL Server table, and is never written to disk. The data is materialized when queried from data available in internal structures maintained by the SQL Server process.

Another way to watch locking activity is with SQL Server Management Studio's Activity Monitor, in the section called **Resource Waits** but, on a very busy system, the performance of the graphical interface can be less than ideal. All the exercises demonstrating locking behavior will use SQL Server Management Studio's query window and most of the examples will select from the `sys.dm_tran_locks` view.

The `sys.dm_tran_locks` view has one row for each lock granted to any session, and one row for each requested lock for which a session is waiting. Each row contains (among other things) the `session_id` of the session holding or waiting for the lock, the lock mode, the lock resource, and the status (granted or waiting). On receiving a new lock request, SQL Server's Lock Manager will examine the contents of `sys.dm_tran_locks` to see if another session already holds, or is waiting for, a lock on the same resource, in an incompatible lock mode. If there is an incompatible lock listed in the `sys.dm_tran_locks` view, the new lock will be added with a status of `WAIT`; otherwise, the lock will be granted to the session.

Almost all of the columns in `sys.dm_tran_locks` start with one of two prefixes. In general, the columns whose names begin with `resource_` describe the resource holding the lock or the resource on which the lock is requested. Two rows in the `sys.dm_tran_locks` view indicate lock requests on the same resource only if all the `resource_` columns are the same.

The columns whose names begin with `request_` describe the requesting session, along with the mode of lock requested, and so on.

Resource columns

Six of the columns in `sys.dm_tran_locks` have the `resource_` prefix, and of these `resource_type` and `resource_description` are probably the most useful, providing the target resource for the requested lock (key, page, and so on) and the identity of the actual resource locked.

There is also a column called `resource_database_id` whose meaning should be obvious, so I won't include it in the subsequent discussion. I will mention, however, that this column returns a numerical value, and we have to translate that number to a database name, using the conversion: `SELECT db_name(<resource_database_id>)`.

Table 2-1 shows many of the possible values for `resource_type`, as well as describing the information returned in the corresponding `resource_description` column.

Resource_Type	Resource_Description	Example
DATABASE	None; the database is always indicated in the `resource_database_ID` column for every locked resource.	
OBJECT	The object ID (which can be any database object, not necessarily a table) is reported in the `resource_associated_entity_id` column.	69575286
HOBT (a partition of a table or index)	None; the `partition_id` is reported in the `resource_associated_entity_id` column.	
EXTENT	File number:page number of the first page of the extent.	1:96
PAGE	File number:page number of the actual table or index page.	1:104
KEY (a row of an index, either clustered or non-clustered)	A hashed value derived from all the key components and the locator. For a non-clustered index on a heap, where columns c1 and c2 are indexed, the hash will contain contributions from c1, c2, and the RID.	ac0001a10a00

Resource_Type	Resource_Description	Example
RID **(a row in a heap)**	File number:pagenumber:slot number of the actual row.	1:161:3
APPLICATION	A concatenation of the database principal with access to this lock, the first 32 characters of the name given to the lock, and a hashed value derived from the full name given to the lock.	0:[ProcLock]:(8e14701f)

Table 2-1: Many of the possible values for resource_type in sys.dm_tran_locks.

Note that key locks and key-range locks both use KEY as the resource description because key range is considered a mode of locking, not a locking resource. However, in the output from the sys.dm_tran_locks view, we can distinguish between these types of locks by the value in the request_mode column.

For locked resources that are part of a larger entity, the resource_associated_entity_id column in sys.dm_tran_locks displays the ID of that associated entity in the database.

The value in this column depends on the resource type:

- ObjectID – The value given in this column for OBJECT resources

- PartitionID – The value provided for resource types PAGE, KEY, RID, and HOBT (note that HOBT is just another way of referring to one partition of a table or index)

- AllocationUnitID – Given for ALLOCATION_UNIT resources.

Of course, for some resources, such as DATABASE and EXTENT, there is no resource_associated_entity_id.

In our queries, we can "decode" the identity of the associated entities on which locks are requested or held, in the current database, by joining `sys.dm_tran_locks` to `sys.partitions`. Listing 2-2 shows how to do this, and wraps the `SELECT` into a view, called `DBLocks`, so that we can reuse it throughout the book.

```
IF EXISTS ( SELECT  1
              FROM    sys.views
              WHERE   name = 'DBlocks' )
    DROP VIEW DBlocks ;
GO
CREATE VIEW DBlocks AS
SELECT  request_session_id AS spid ,
        DB_NAME(resource_database_id) AS dbname ,
        CASE WHEN resource_type = 'OBJECT'
             THEN OBJECT_NAME(resource_associated_entity_id)
             WHEN resource_associated_entity_id = 0 THEN 'n/a'
             ELSE OBJECT_NAME(p.object_id)
        END AS entity_name ,
        index_id ,
        resource_type AS resource ,
        resource_description AS description ,
        request_mode AS mode ,
        request_status AS status
 FROM    sys.dm_tran_locks t
         LEFT JOIN sys.partitions p
                   ON p.partition_id = t.resource_associated_entity_id
 WHERE   resource_database_id = DB_ID()
         AND resource_type <> 'DATABASE' ;
```

Listing 2-2:   Creation of the `DBLocks` view to display locks in the current database.

For `OBJECT` resources, we apply the `object_name` function to the `resource_associated_entity_id` column. For `PAGE`, `KEY`, and `RID` resources, we use the `object_name` function, with the `ObjectID` from the `sys.partitions` view. There is no simple function to convert a `HOBT ID` value to an object name; we have to select from the `sys.partitions` view. For other resources for which there is no `resource_associated_entity_id`, the code just returns n/a.

The `object_name` function applies only to the current database, so the `WHERE` clause filters to return only lock information for resources in the current database. The organization of the output reflects the information returned by the `sp_lockprocedure`, but we can add any additional filters or columns, as required. We'll use this view in many examples later in this book.

Request columns

There are 13 columns in `sys.dm_tran_locks` used to identify information about the request for the lock, but two of them are documented as being *for informational purposes only, not supported*. Another two are only useful for DTC transactions or transactions using the MARS protocol, we won't discuss them further. Below is a list of the other nine with a basic explanation of their meaning.

- **request_mode** – This is the lock mode discussed earlier, and indicates whether the granted or requested lock is shared (S), exclusive (X), intent shared (IX), update (U), and so on. Key-range locks, used for `SERIALIZABLE` isolation, appear as `RangeS-U`, `RangeS-S` and so on (see Chapter 3). For granted requests, this is the granted mode; for waiting requests, this is the mode being requested.

- **request_type** – In SQL Server 2008, the only type of resource request tracked in `sys.dm_tran_locks` is for a `LOCK`. Future versions will include other types of resources that can be requested.

- **request_status** – Status can be one of three values: `GRANT`, `CONVERT`, or `WAIT`. A status of `CONVERT` indicates that the requestor has already been granted a request for the same resource in a different mode and is currently waiting for an upgrade (convert) from the current lock mode to be granted. (For example, SQL Server can convert a U lock to X.) A status of `WAIT` indicates that the requestor does not currently hold a granted request on the resource.

- **request_session_id** – This value is the ID of the session that has requested the lock. The owning session ID can change for distributed (DTC) and bound transactions.

- **request_reference_count** – This value is a rough count of the number of times the same requestor has requested this resource, and applies only to resources that are not automatically released at the end of a transaction.

- **request_exec_context_id** – This value is the execution context ID of the process that currently owns this request. A value greater than 0 indicates that this is a sub-thread used to execute a parallel query.

- **request_owner_type** – This value refers to the owner discussed earlier, which indicates the scope of the lock. The five possible values are: TRANSACTION, SHARED_TRANSACTION_WORKSPACE, EXCLUSIVE_TRANSACTION_WORKSPACE, CURSOR and SESSION.

- **request_owner_id** – This value is currently used only for requests with an owner of TRANSACTION, and the owner ID is the transaction ID. This column can be joined with the transaction_id column in the sys.dm_tran_active_transactions view.

- **lock_owner_address** – This value is the memory address of the internal data structure that is used to track this request. This column can be joined with the resource_address column in sys.dm_os_waiting_tasks if this request is in the WAIT or CONVERT state.

Locking Examples

The following examples show what many of the lock types and lock resources look like when reported using the DBLocks view from Listing 2-2. The more familiar we are with querying the locking metadata and studying the output, the better we'll be able to troubleshoot any blocking problems that may arise.

Example 1: SELECT with READ COMMITTED isolation level

The script in Listing 2-3 begins a **READ COMMITTED** transaction, queries the `Production.Product` table, and then immediately interrogates our **DBLocks** view.

```
USE AdventureWorks ;
SET TRANSACTION ISOLATION LEVEL READ COMMITTED ;
BEGIN TRAN
SELECT   *
FROM     Production.Product
WHERE    Name = 'Reflector' ;
SELECT   *
FROM     DBlocks
WHERE    spid = @@spid ;
COMMIT TRAN
```

Listing 2-3:   A simple **SELECT** in **READ COMMITTED** isolation level.

There are no locks on the data in the `Production.Product` table because the batch was doing only **SELECT** operations, and so acquired only S locks. By default, SQL Server releases S locks as soon as it has finished reading the data so, by the time we execute the **SELECT** from the view, SQL Server no longer holds the locks. As such, the results in Figure 2-1 show only an **OBJECT** lock on the view (there is also a **DATABASE** lock on the `AdventureWorks` database, but the **DBLocks** view filtered out database locks).

	spid	dbname	entity_name	index_id	resource	description	mode	status
1	55	AdventureWorks	DBlocks	NULL	OBJECT		IS	GRANT

Figure 2-1:   Locks held during simple **SELECT** in **READ COMMITTED** isolation level.

Example 2: SELECT with REPEATABLE READ isolation level

In Listing 2-4, we run another query against `Production.Product`, as part of a **REPEATABLE READ** transaction. This time, we filter out the lock on the view so that we can focus just on the data locks.

```
USE AdventureWorks ;
SET TRANSACTION ISOLATION LEVEL REPEATABLE READ ;
BEGIN TRAN
SELECT  *
FROM    Production.Product
WHERE   Name LIKE 'Racing Socks%' ;
SELECT  *
FROM    DBlocks
WHERE   spid = @@spid
        AND entity_name = 'Product' ;
COMMIT TRAN
```

Listing 2-4:   A simple SELECT in REPEATABLE READ isolation level.

This time, because the transaction isolation level is **REPEATABLE READ**, SQL Server holds the S locks until the transaction is finished and so we can see them in our results. The `Production.Product` table has a clustered index, so the rows of data are all index rows in the leaf level. As such, Figure 2-2 shows that the locks on the two individual data rows returned are KEY locks. The table also has a non-clustered index on the `Name` column and we can see two KEY locks at the leaf level of this non-clustered index, used to find the relevant rows.

We can distinguish the clustered and non-clustered indexes by the value in the `Index_ID` column: the data rows have an `Index_id` value of 1, and the non-clustered index rows have an `Index_ID` value of 3 (the `index_id` value for non-clustered indexes can be any number between 2 and 999).

Note that all these index rows have S locks, and the data and index pages, as well as the table itself, have IS locks.

	spid	dbname	entity_name	index_id	resource	description	mode	status
1	52	AdventureWorks	Product	NULL	OBJECT		IS	GRANT
2	52	AdventureWorks	Product	1	PAGE	1:9057	IS	GRANT
3	52	AdventureWorks	Product	1	KEY	(6b00b8eeda30)	S	GRANT
4	52	AdventureWorks	Product	1	KEY	(6a00dd896688)	S	GRANT
5	52	AdventureWorks	Product	3	PAGE	1:4606	IS	GRANT
6	52	AdventureWorks	Product	3	KEY	(9502d56a217e)	S	GRANT
7	52	AdventureWorks	Product	3	KEY	(9602945b3a67)	S	GRANT

Figure 2-2:   Locks held during simple SELECT in REPEATABLE READ isolation level.

Example 3: SELECT with SERIALIZABLE isolation level

Listing 2-5 repeats the previous example, except with the use of the SERIALIZABLE transaction isolation level.

```
USE AdventureWorks ;
SET TRANSACTION ISOLATION LEVEL SERIALIZABLE ;
BEGIN TRAN
SELECT  *
FROM    Production.Product
WHERE   Name LIKE 'Racing Socks%' ;
SELECT  *
FROM    DBlocks
WHERE   spid = @@spid
        AND entity_name = 'Product' ;
COMMIT TRAN
```

Listing 2-5:   A simple SELECT in SERIALIZABLE isolation level.

The locks held with the **SERIALIZABLE** isolation level are almost identical to those held with the **REPEATABLE READ** isolation level. As such, the results, shown in Figure 2-3 show many similarities to the previous results, in the form of the S-mode **KEY** locks on the rows in the clustered index, and in the IS locks on the parent pages and object. However, the primary difference is the number and mode of the locks on the rows in the non-clustered index.

	spid	dbname	entity_name	index_id	resource	description	mode	status
1	52	AdventureWorks	Product	NULL	OBJECT		IS	GRANT
2	52	AdventureWorks	Product	1	PAGE	1:9057	IS	GRANT
3	52	AdventureWorks	Product	1	KEY	(6b00b8eeda30)	S	GRANT
4	52	AdventureWorks	Product	1	KEY	(6a00dd896688)	S	GRANT
5	52	AdventureWorks	Product	3	PAGE	1:4606	IS	GRANT
6	52	AdventureWorks	Product	3	KEY	(9502d56a217e)	RangeS-S	GRANT
7	52	AdventureWorks	Product	3	KEY	(23027a50f6db)	RangeS-S	GRANT
8	52	AdventureWorks	Product	3	KEY	(9602945b3a67)	RangeS-S	GRANT

Figure 2-3: Locks held during simple **SELECT** in **SERIALIZABLE** isolation level.

The two-part mode **RangeS-S** indicates a key-range lock in addition to the lock on the key itself. The first part (**RangeS**) is the lock on the range of keys between and including the key holding the lock and the previous key in the index. The key-range locks prevent other transactions from inserting any new rows into the table that meet the condition of this query; that is, it's not possible to insert any new rows with a product name starting with **Racing Socks**. The key-range locks are held on ranges in the non-clustered index on **Name** (**Index_id** = 3) because that is the index used to find the qualifying rows.

The two Racing Socks rows are **Racing Socks, L** and **Racing Socks, M**. There are three **KEY** locks in the non-clustered index because SQL Server must lock three different ranges of data, as follows:

• the range from the key preceding the first Racing Socks row in the index (which is **Pinch Bolt**) up to the first Racing Socks row (**Racing Socks, L**)

- the range between the two rows starting with Racing Socks

- The range from the second Racing Socks row (`Racing Socks, M`) to the next key in the index (`Rear Brakes`).

So, in fact, while this transaction is in progress no other transaction could insert rows anywhere between `Pinch Bolt` and `Rear Brakes`. For example, we could not insert a product with the name `Port Key` or `Racing Tights`.

Example 4: Update with READ COMMITTED isolation level

In this example, we move on to an **UPDATE** operation, running under the default **READ COMMITTED** isolation level (the default), as shown in Listing 2-6.

```
USE AdventureWorks ;
SET TRANSACTION ISOLATION LEVEL READ COMMITTED ;
BEGIN TRAN
UPDATE   Production.Product
SET      ListPrice = ListPrice * 0.6
WHERE    Name LIKE 'Racing Socks%' ;
SELECT   *
FROM     DBlocks
WHERE    spid = @@spid
         AND entity_name = 'Product' ;
COMMIT TRAN
```

Listing 2-6:   A simple UPDATE in READ COMMITTED isolation level.

Figure 2-4 shows that the two rows in the leaf level of the clustered index are locked with X locks. The page and the table are then locked with IX locks.

	spid	dbname	entity_name	index_id	resource	description	mode	status
1	52	AdventureWorks	Product	NULL	OBJECT		IX	GRANT
2	52	AdventureWorks	Product	1	KEY	(6b00b8eeda30)	X	GRANT
3	52	AdventureWorks	Product	1	KEY	(6a00dd896688)	X	GRANT
4	52	AdventureWorks	Product	1	PAGE	1:9057	IX	GRANT

Figure 2-4: Locks held during a simple UPDATE in READ COMMITTED isolation level.

As discussed earlier, SQL Server acquires U locks while it looks for the rows to update. However, SQL Server escalates these to X locks upon performing the actual update and, by the time we look at the DBLocks view, the U locks are gone. Unless we force U locks with a query hint, we might never see them in the lock report from DBLocks, or by direct inspection of sys.dm_tran_locks.

Example 5: Update with SERIALIZABLE isolation level (with an index)

In this example, we rerun the same UPDATE as for Example 4, but using the SERIALIZABLE isolation level, as shown in Listing 2-7.

```
USE AdventureWorks ;
SET TRANSACTION ISOLATION LEVEL SERIALIZABLE ;
BEGIN TRAN
UPDATE   Production.Product
SET      ListPrice = ListPrice * 0.6
WHERE    Name LIKE 'Racing Socks%' ;
SELECT   *
FROM     DBlocks
WHERE    spid = @@spid
         AND entity_name = 'Product' ;
COMMIT TRAN
```

Listing 2-7: A simple UPDATE in SERIALIZABLE isolation level, using an index.

Again, notice that the key-range locks are on the non-clustered index, used to find the relevant rows. The range interval itself needs only an S lock to prevent insertions, but the searched keys have U locks, ensuring that no other process can attempt to UPDATE them. The keys in the table itself (index_id = 1) obtain the X lock when the actual modification is made.

	spid	dbname	entity_name	index_id	resource	description	mode	status
1	52	AdventureWorks	Product	NULL	OBJECT		IX	GRANT
2	52	AdventureWorks	Product	1	PAGE	1:9057	IX	GRANT
3	52	AdventureWorks	Product	1	KEY	(6b00b8eeda30)	X	GRANT
4	52	AdventureWorks	Product	1	KEY	(6a00dd896688)	X	GRANT
5	52	AdventureWorks	Product	3	PAGE	1:4606	IU	GRANT
6	52	AdventureWorks	Product	3	KEY	(9502d56a217e)	RangeS-U	GRANT
7	52	AdventureWorks	Product	3	KEY	(23027a50f6db)	RangeS-U	GRANT
8	52	AdventureWorks	Product	3	KEY	(9602945b3a67)	RangeS-U	GRANT

Figure 2-5: Locks held during a simple UPDATE in SERIALIZABLE isolation level, using an index.

Example 6: Update with SERIALIZABLE isolation level not using an index

Now let's look at another UPDATE operation with the SERIALIZABLE isolation level, but there is no useful index for the search, as shown in Listing 2-8.

```
USE AdventureWorks ;
SET TRANSACTION ISOLATION LEVEL SERIALIZABLE ;
BEGIN TRAN
UPDATE   Production.Product
SET      ListPrice = ListPrice * 0.6
WHERE    Color = 'White' ;
SELECT   *
FROM     DBlocks
WHERE    spid = @@spid
         AND entity_name = 'Product' ;
COMMIT TRAN
```

Listing 2-8: A simple UPDATE in SERIALIZABLE isolation level, not using an index.

The locks in Figure 2-6 are similar to those in Figure 2-5 except that all the locks are on the table itself (`Index_Id` = 1).

387	52	AdventureWorks	Product	1	KEY	(7800a7c2f271)	RangeS-U	GRANT
388	52	AdventureWorks	Product	1	KEY	(0a00de7e40b3)	RangeS-U	GRANT
389	52	AdventureWorks	Product	1	KEY	(74001f7d243b)	RangeS-U	GRANT
390	52	AdventureWorks	Product	1	KEY	(7e0015491d57)	RangeS-U	GRANT
391	52	AdventureWorks	Product	1	KEY	(7200adf6cb1d)	RangeS-U	GRANT
392	52	AdventureWorks	Product	1	KEY	(66006536b0c2)	RangeS-U	GRANT
393	52	AdventureWorks	Product	1	KEY	(03000d8f0ecc)	RangeS-U	GRANT
394	52	AdventureWorks	Product	1	KEY	(6a00dd896688)	RangeX-X	GRANT
395	52	AdventureWorks	Product	1	KEY	(ac0069ecc4d8)	RangeS-U	GRANT
396	52	AdventureWorks	Product	1	KEY	(c500b9eaac9c)	RangeX-X	GRANT
397	52	AdventureWorks	Product	1	KEY	(d200a8efa050)	RangeS-U	GRANT
398	52	AdventureWorks	Product	1	KEY	(a000d1531292)	RangeS-U	GRANT
399	52	AdventureWorks	Product	1	KEY	(c90001557ad6)	RangeS-U	GRANT
400	52	AdventureWorks	Product	1	KEY	(de0010507f1a)	RangeS-U	GRANT

Figure 2-6: Some of the locks held during a simple UPDATE in SERIALIZABLE isolation level, not using an index.

As there was no useful index, a clustered index scan on the entire table was required, and so all keys initially received the **RangeS-U** lock; when four rows were eventually modified, the locks on those keys escalated to the **RangeX-X** lock. We can see two of the **RangeX-X** locks, and a few of the **RangeS-U** locks. The complete output has 501 **RangeS-U** locks, as well as IU locks on several pages, IX locks on two pages, and an IX lock on the table.

Example 7: Creating a table

Let's now investigate locking behavior as we create a new table, as part of transaction using **READ COMMITTED** transaction isolation.

```
USE AdventureWorks ;
SET TRANSACTION ISOLATION LEVEL READ COMMITTED ;
BEGIN TRAN
SELECT   *
INTO     newProducts
FROM     Production.Product
WHERE    ListPrice BETWEEN 1 AND 10 ;
SELECT   *
FROM     DBlocks
WHERE    spid = @@spid ;
COMMIT TRAN
```

Listing 2-9: Creating a new table using SELECT...INTO.

Figure 2-7 shows that SQL Server acquired very few of these locks on elements of the
newProducts table. In the entity_name column, note that most of the objects are
undocumented, and normally invisible, system table names. When creating the new table,
SQL Server acquires locks on six different system tables to record information about
this new table. In addition, notice the schema modification (Sch-M) locks which we'll be
discussing in the section on lock compatibility, in Chapter 3.

	spid	dbname	entity_name	index_id	resource	description	mode	status
1	52	AdventureWorks	n/a	NULL	METADATA	user_type_id = 258	Sch-S	GRANT
2	52	AdventureWorks	n/a	NULL	METADATA	data_space_id = 1	Sch-S	GRANT
3	52	AdventureWorks	n/a	NULL	METADATA	user_type_id = 260	Sch-S	GRANT
4	52	AdventureWorks	n/a	NULL	METADATA	$seq_type = 0, object_id = 297768118	Sch-M	GRANT
5	52	AdventureWorks	sysrscols	NULL	OBJECT		IX	GRANT
6	52	AdventureWorks	sysrowsets	NULL	OBJECT		IX	GRANT
7	52	AdventureWorks	sysallocunits	NULL	OBJECT		IX	GRANT
8	52	AdventureWorks	sysschobjs	NULL	OBJECT		IX	GRANT
9	52	AdventureWorks	syscolpars	NULL	OBJECT		IX	GRANT
10	52	AdventureWorks	sysidxstats	NULL	OBJECT		IX	GRANT
11	52	AdventureWorks	sysrscols	1	KEY	(17002bfdc1fa)	X	GRANT
12	52	AdventureWorks	sysrscols	1	KEY	(0300e33dba25)	X	GRANT
13	52	AdventureWorks	sysrscols	1	KEY	(0f005b826c6f)	X	GRANT
14	52	AdventureWorks	sysrscols	1	KEY	(1500a035c850)	X	GRANT
15	52	AdventureWorks	sysrscols	1	KEY	(1900188a1e1a)	X	GRANT
16	52	AdventureWorks	sysrscols	1	KEY	(0d00d04a65c5)	X	GRANT
17	52	AdventureWorks	sysrscols	1	KEY	(010068f5b38f)	X	GRANT

Figure 2-7: Some of the locks held during a table creation using SELECT...INTO.

Example 8: RID locks

Our last example will look at the locks held when there is no clustered index on the table and a transaction updates the data rows, as shown in Listing 2-10.

```
USE AdventureWorks ;
SET TRANSACTION ISOLATION LEVEL READ COMMITTED
BEGIN TRAN
UPDATE    newProducts
SET       ListPrice = 5.99
WHERE     name = 'Road Bottle Cage' ;
SELECT    *
FROM      DBlocks
WHERE     spid = @@spid
          AND entity_name = 'newProducts' ;
COMMIT TRAN
```

Listing 2-10: Updating rows in a heap.

There are no indexes on the `newProducts` table, so the lock on the actual row meeting our criterion is an X lock on the row (RID). For `RID` locks, the description actually reports the specific row in the form **File Number:Page number:Slot number**. As expected, SQL Server takes IX locks on the page and the table.

	spid	dbname	entity_name	index_id	resource	description	mode	status
1	52	AdventureWorks	newProducts	NULL	OBJECT		IX	GRANT
2	52	AdventureWorks	newProducts	0	RID	1:46756:5	X	GRANT
3	52	AdventureWorks	newProducts	0	PAGE	1:46756	IX	GRANT

Figure 2-8: Locks held when updating rows in a heap.

Summary

In this chapter, we looked at the basics of SQL Server's default locking behavior; the types of locks that SQL Server can acquire, the granularity of the lock, and the duration of the locks. We saw how the locking behavior changes, depending on the transaction isolation level, in order to enforce the behaviors required by the definition of the isolation level. Finally, we looked at multiple examples of locking in various transactions, and examined the locks acquired using SQL Server's lock metadata.

Chapter 3: Advanced Locking Concepts

A session wishing to access a particular resource may be blocked, and forced to wait, if the required resource is unavailable. By far the most common type of resource to have to wait for is a lock. In other words, another session already holds a lock on the required resource, with which the requested lock is incompatible, so forcing the requesting sessions to wait until the holding session releases the lock.

The previous chapter briefly introduced the various modes of lock that SQL Server can acquire, including shared (S) locks, exclusive (X) locks, and update (U) locks. Here, we'll take a deeper look at how and when SQL Server acquires these, and other "specialized" types of locks, on various resources, covering concepts such as:

- **lock compatibility** – which lock types are compatible, and so can exist simultaneously on the same resource, and which are incompatible, and so will lead to blocking

- **lock mode conversion** – how SQL Server converts lock modes in response to the operations being performed by a given transaction, in order to ensure enforcement of the ACID transaction properties

- **special intent locks** – acquired when a non-intent lock is requested on a resource on which either an IX or an IU lock is already held

- **key-range locks** – introduced in Chapter 2 as a type of lock acquired in SERIALIZABLE isolation level when scanning or modifying a range of data; here, we take a closer look at the four most common modes of key-range lock.

Where a choice exists, SQL Server will always acquire locks at the lowest level of granularity (e.g. on a row rather than a page), but there are times when it may opt to **escalate** the locks for a given session, on a specific resource, to the table level. We'll examine the circumstances in which this might happen, and how we might exert some control over it.

Finally, we end the chapter with some "lesser-known" lock types that can occasionally rear their heads and cause unexpected blocking issues, namely, latches and compile locks.

Lock Compatibility

If a session requests a lock, SQL Server inspects the locks currently held (which we can see in the `sys.dm_tran_locks` view) to see if another session holds a lock on the exact same resource. SQL Server performs a check for lock compatibility only if it already holds locks on the requested resource. Internally, SQL Server maintains a list of which lock types are compatible with other types, and if existing and requested lock types are compatible, SQL Server grants the requested lock. If the requested lock is of a type that is incompatible, SQL Server gives the requested lock a status of 'WAIT'. SQL Server Books Online provides a lock compatibility matrix, which I have reproduced in Table 3-1.

Requested lock mode	Existing granted lock mode				
	IS	S	U	IX	X
Intent shared (IS)	Yes	Yes	Yes	Yes	No
Shared (S)	Yes	Yes	Yes	No	No
Update (U)	Yes	Yes	No	No	No
Intent exclusive (IX)	Yes	No	No	Yes	No
Exclusive (X)	No	No	No	No	No

Table 3-1: Lock compatibility matrix.

To determine the compatibility, find the existing lock along the top and look down that column. Find the requested lock type along the left and look across that row. The place where the row and column meet reveals the compatibility.

For example, suppose `Session1` has an exclusive lock on a row in `TableA`. Can `Session2` get an exclusive lock on another row in `TableA`? `Session1` has an X lock on a row, but `Session2` is not trying to lock the same row, so there will be no conflict there. Remember, though, that when `Session1` gets an X lock on the row in `TableA`, it will also get an intent exclusive lock (IX) on the page containing the row, and on the table containing the row, which is `TableA`. There is no existing lock on the row that `Session2` wants, so `Session2` can get the X lock on the row, the IX lock on the page and an IX lock on `TableA`. Notice, in the lock compatibility chart above, that IX locks are *compatible* with other IX locks, and hopefully this example explains why that is a good thing.

Now suppose `Session3` wants an exclusive lock on the *same* row that `Session1` is locking. SQL Server actually attempts to acquire the higher-level locks first. So `Session3` will be able to get the IX lock on `TableA` and the IX lock on the page, but it will not be able to get the lock on the row, because `Session1` already has an X lock on the row, and in the lock compatibility matrix, X locks are *incompatible* with X locks.

In addition to the compatibilities indicated in the lock compatibility matrix, three more lock modes have compatibility issues of which we should be aware.

- **Sch-S – schema stability lock**
  SQL Server acquires a Sch-S lock whenever it is compiling and optimizing a query. Sch-S locks are the most compatible of all the lock modes, and do not block on any transactional locks, including X locks. It's perfectly fine for one session to be modifying data in a table while SQL Server is optimizing a query for another session that is accessing that table. The only lock mode that will block Sch-S locks is Sch-M, described next.

- **Sch-M – schema modification lock**
  SQL Server acquires a Sch-M lock when performing certain DDL operations that change a table's definition (its schema). These operations include adding and dropping columns from the table, or changing a column's data type. Sch-M locks are the least compatible lock mode and a request for every other mode will block on a Sch-M lock, and vice versa; a session cannot get a Sch-M lock if any other session has any other lock on the table. In other words, when a session is making a schema change to a table, no other sessions can do anything with the table.

- **BU – bulk update lock**
  SQL Server acquires a BU lock on a table only if a session explicitly requests one, during a bulk insert operation into the table. With the **BULK INSERT** command we can specify a BU lock, using the **TABLOCK** hint, and with the **bcp** utility we can use the **–h "TABLOCK"** option. We can specify that SQL Server take BU locks, by default, for a particular table, during bulk updates, via use of the **sp_tableoption** system stored procedure, with the **table lock on bulk load** option enabled. BU locks allow multiple threads to load data into the same table concurrently, and they are only compatible with other BU locks and with Sch-S locks. Bulk load operations that do not request the BU lock use normal row-level X locks, as the new rows are added.

Lock Mode Conversion

The lock mode is determined primarily by the operation being performed. S locks are acquired when reading (selecting) data, and X locks are acquired when writing (or modifying) data. X locks will never change to S locks, but an S lock could change to an X lock, if a new operation is performed on the same resource, in the same transaction.

We can run the script in Listing 3-1 to see this transformation, from S to X lock, in action.

```
USE AdventureWorks;
-- Create a new table
IF OBJECTPROPERTY(OBJECT_ID('NewOrders'), 'IsUserTable') = 1
    DROP TABLE NewOrders;
GO
SELECT  *
INTO    NewOrders
FROM    Sales.SalesOrderHeader;
GO
CREATE UNIQUE INDEX NewOrder_index ON NewOrders(SalesOrderID);
GO

-- Change isolation level and start transaction
SET TRANSACTION ISOLATION LEVEL REPEATABLE READ;
BEGIN TRAN

-- SELECT data and examine the locks
SELECT  *
FROM    NewOrders
WHERE   SalesOrderID = 55555;

SELECT  *
FROM    DBlocks
WHERE   spid = @@spid
        AND entity_name = 'NewOrders';

-- UPDATE data and examine the locks
UPDATE  NewOrders
SET     SalesPersonID = 277
WHERE   SalesOrderID = 55555;

SELECT  *
FROM    DBlocks
WHERE   spid = @@spid
        AND entity_name = 'NewOrders';

ROLLBACK TRAN
```

Listing 3-1:   Lock conversion from S to X.

The code in Listing 3-1 will drop the NewOrders table if it already exists, then re-create it and build a non-clustered index on the SalesOrderID column. It then sets the isolation level to REPEATABLE READ in order that SQL Server holds S locks until the end of the transaction rather than just the end of the current statement, as is the case in the default READ COMMITTED level.

The code then opens a REPEATABLE READ transaction and selects one row from the NewOrders table. When querying our DBLocks view (see Chapter 2), we see an S lock on a RID in the database. This is the RID for the row that was selected, with SalesOrderID = 55555. Also, note that an S lock is held for a key in the non-clustered index. There are also IS locks for the page in the table that contains the selected row, and for the page in the index that contains the key for the selected row as well as an IS lock on the table itself.

After we update the row, we query the DBLocks view again, and this time there are different locks on the same resources. The same RID now has an X lock, and the page in the table, and the table itself, both have IX locks. The key in the index has a U lock. SQL Server acquired the U lock while searching for the row to update, and this is necessary because, until the modification to the data row happens, SQL Server doesn't know whether the modification will also require a change to the index. The page in the index containing the key has an IU lock. Figure 3-1 shows the results, revealing all these locks.

	SalesOrderID	RevisionNumber	OrderDate	DueDate	ShipDate
1	55555	2	2003-10-05 ...	2003-10-17...	2003-10-12 00:00:00.000

	spid	dbname	entity_name	index_id	resource	description	mode	status
1	55	AdventureWorks	NewOrders	NULL	OBJECT		IS	GRANT
2	55	AdventureWorks	NewOrders	0	PAGE	1:70144	IS	GRANT
3	55	AdventureWorks	NewOrders	0	RID	1:70144:30	S	GRANT
4	55	AdventureWorks	NewOrders	2	KEY	(0300b2...	S	GRANT
5	55	AdventureWorks	NewOrders	2	PAGE	1:70886	IS	GRANT

	spid	dbname	entity_name	index_id	resource	description	mode	status
1	55	AdventureWorks	NewOrders	NULL	OBJECT		IX	GRANT
2	55	AdventureWorks	NewOrders	0	PAGE	1:70144	IX	GRANT
3	55	AdventureWorks	NewOrders	0	RID	1:70144:30	X	GRANT
4	55	AdventureWorks	NewOrders	2	KEY	(0300b2...	U	GRANT
5	55	AdventureWorks	NewOrders	2	PAGE	1:70886	IU	GRANT

Figure 3-1:   Locks acquired by a SELECT and then UPDATE in the same transaction.

Special Intent Locks

As described earlier, when discussing different lock modes, SQL Server acquires an intent lock on a high-level resource when it holds a lock on a component of that resource. In Listing 3-1, we saw that when SQL Server holds an S lock on a row, then it also holds IS locks on the page and the table containing that row. SQL Server acquires an IU lock on an index page, when the component (a key) of that index had a U lock. In addition to the IS, IX, and IU locks we saw in Listing 3-1, there are three more types of intent locks that can be considered **conversion locks**. SQL Server will acquire these types of lock when a non-intent lock is requested on a resource on which either an IX or an IU lock is already held.

Note that these three types of locks will only occur when SQL Server acquires both an intent and a non-intent lock on the same resource. If two intent locks are requested, the stronger one will always replace the weaker one. For example, if a page had an IU lock and then an IX lock was requested, the IX lock would simply replace the IU lock.

Listing 3-2 shows a script, similar to the one in Listing 3-1, which will demonstrate the acquisition of each of these special intent locks. Take a look now, and execute the relevant step as we work through each of the three types.

```
USE AdventureWorks;
--Step 1:  Create a new table and set the isolation level
IF OBJECTPROPERTY(OBJECT_ID('NewOrders'), 'IsUserTable') = 1
    DROP TABLE NewOrders;
GO
SELECT  *
INTO    NewOrders
FROM    Sales.SalesOrderHeader;
GO
CREATE UNIQUE INDEX NewOrder_index ON NewOrders(SalesOrderID);
GO
SET TRANSACTION ISOLATION LEVEL SERIALIZABLE;
GO


-- Step 2: Generate an SIX lock
BEGIN TRAN
UPDATE  dbo.NewOrders
SET     ShipDate = ShipDate + 1
WHERE   SalesOrderID = 55555;
GO
SELECT  *
FROM    DBlocks
WHERE   spid = @@spid
        AND entity_name = 'NewOrders';
GO
SELECT  *
FROM    dbo.NewOrders WITH ( TABLOCK, REPEATABLEREAD )
WHERE   SalesOrderID = 55555;
GO
SELECT  *
FROM    DBlocks
```

```
WHERE    spid = @@spid
         AND entity_name = 'NewOrders';
GO
ROLLBACK TRAN
GO

-- Step 3: Generate an UIX lock
BEGIN TRAN
UPDATE   dbo.NewOrders
SET      ShipDate = ShipDate + 1
WHERE    SalesOrderID = 55555;
GO
SELECT   *
FROM     DBlocks
WHERE    spid = @@spid
         AND entity_name = 'NewOrders';
GO
SELECT   *
FROM     dbo.NewOrders WITH ( PAGLOCK, UPDLOCK )
WHERE    SalesOrderID = 55555;
GO
SELECT   *
FROM     DBlocks
WHERE    spid = @@spid
         AND entity_name = 'NewOrders';
GO
ROLLBACK TRAN
GO

-- Step 4: Generate an SIU lock
BEGIN TRAN
UPDATE   dbo.NewOrders
SET      ShipDate = ShipDate + 1
WHERE    SalesOrderID = 55555;
GO
SELECT   *
FROM     DBlocks
WHERE    spid = @@spid
         AND entity_name = 'NewOrders';
GO
SELECT   *
FROM     dbo.NewOrders WITH ( PAGLOCK, REPEATABLEREAD )
WHERE    SalesOrderID = 55555;
GO
```

```
SELECT  *
FROM    DBlocks
WHERE   spid = @@spid
        AND entity_name = 'NewOrders';
GO
ROLLBACK TRAN
GO
```

Listing 3-2:   Generating special intent locks.

Execute Step 1 in Listing 3-2 now, so that we start with a clean table.

Shared intent exclusive (SIX)

When SQL Server has one or more rows locked with X locks, the pages and the table that contains the rows will acquire IX locks. When the same transaction performs an operation that requires an S lock, SQL Server will acquire a SIX lock on the table.

Step 2 in Listing 3-2 starts with the **UPDATE** statement, which will acquire an X lock on the updated row, and IX locks on the page and the table containing the row. The subsequent query against the **NewOrders** table, in the same transaction, will obtain an S lock on the table and hold it to the end of the transaction, thanks to the **REPEATABLE READ** hint. The query against the **DBLocks** view reveals that SQL Server has acquired an SIX lock on the table.

Note that, even though the **SELECT** statement on the **NewOrders** table is accessing every row in that table, the default is for SQL Server to acquire individual row locks. For the sake of greater concurrency, SQL Server will not automatically escalate row locks into table locks until a very large number of locks are acquired, at which point the overhead of maintaining all those locks outweighs the concurrency benefits. The escalation point is when SQL Server is using about 3% of its memory for keeping track of all its locks.

At that time, SQL Server will try to escalate multiple table locks on the same table into a single table lock, but if other resources (rows or pages) in the table are locked by another session, the escalation will not take place. In that case, SQL Server will continue to use row locks, and possibly acquire more row locks. We'll discuss lock escalation in more detail very shortly.

Update intent exclusive (UIX)

SQL Server never acquires U locks at the table level, so the only way to get a U lock and an IX lock together is on a page. Step 3 in Listing 3-2 illustrates this behavior. We execute the **UPDATE** statement first and, because a row is updated, that row gets an X lock, and the page and table acquire IX locks. When the subsequent **SELECT** is run, with hints forcing U locks on the pages accessed, the U lock on the page combines with the previous IX lock on the page, to give a UIX lock.

Shared intent update (SIU)

SQL Server holds IU locks only at the page level; the corresponding table will have an IX lock. To see an SIU lock, we can run a query that acquires a U lock on a row, so it will also acquire an IU lock on the page. If, in the same transaction, we then acquire an S lock on the page, the result will be an SIU lock. Step 4 in Listing 3-2 shows this behavior.

Key-Range Locks

We briefly discussed key-range locks in Chapter 2, when considering lock resources and **SERIALIZABLE** isolation level. If the isolation level is **SERIALIZABLE** and a query scans a range of data within a transaction, SQL Server needs to lock enough of the table to ensure that another transaction cannot insert a new value into the range currently being scanned, because if we reissued the same query that value would then appear as a phantom.

A key-range lock is associated with a specific index key, but includes the range of possible values less than or equal to the key with which the lock is associated, and greater than the previous key in the index leaf level. Another way to say it would be that a key-range lock spans the range between two keys, and includes the key at the end, but not the key at the beginning. For example, if an index leaf level included the sequential values "James" and "Jones," a key-range lock on "Jones" would lock out all key values greater than "James" and less than or equal to "Jones."

Key-range locks appear in the `request_mode` column the `sys.dm_tran_locks` view (or our `DBLocks` view) as a two-part name. The first part of the name indicates the lock on the range (the interval between the two key values), and the second part indicates the lock on the key at the upper end of the range.

SQL Server can hold nine different key-range lock modes, and can only acquire these modes when a transaction is using `SERIALIZABLE` isolation level. However, there are only four frequently observed key-range lock modes. The others are conversion locks, obtained only when SQL Server converts from another lock mode, and are usually so transient that it is difficult to detect them using the tools we have.

We'll focus on the four, more frequently observed key-range lock modes here, and will use the script in Listing 3-3 to generate each of them. Again, take a look at the script, and execute the relevant step in each of the subsequent four sections. Start now, by executing Step 1, to start with a clean table and set the transaction isolation level to `SERIALIZABLE`.

```
USE AdventureWorks;
--Step 1:  Create a new table and set the isolation level
IF OBJECTPROPERTY(OBJECT_ID('NewOrders'), 'IsUserTable') = 1
    DROP TABLE NewOrders;
GO
SELECT  *
INTO    NewOrders
FROM    Sales.SalesOrderHeader;
GO
```

```
CREATE UNIQUE INDEX NewOrder_index ON NewOrders(SalesOrderID);
GO
SET TRANSACTION ISOLATION LEVEL SERIALIZABLE;
GO

-- Step 2: Generate RangeS-S locks
BEGIN TRAN
SELECT  *
FROM    dbo.NewOrders
WHERE   SalesOrderID BETWEEN 55555 AND 55557;
GO
SELECT  *
FROM    DBlocks
WHERE   spid = @@spid
        AND entity_name = 'NewOrders';
GO
ROLLBACK TRAN
GO


-- Step 3: Generate RangeS-U locks

BEGIN TRAN
UPDATE  dbo.NewOrders
SET     ShipDate = ShipDate + 1
WHERE   SalesOrderID BETWEEN 55555 AND 55557;
GO
SELECT  *
FROM    DBlocks
WHERE   spid = @@spid
        AND entity_name = 'NewOrders';
GO
ROLLBACK TRAN

-- STEP 4: Generate RangeX-X locks
-- We need a clustered index to see these locks
CREATE UNIQUE CLUSTERED INDEX NewOrder_index ON NewOrders(SalesOrderID)
WITH DROP_EXISTING;
GO
BEGIN TRAN
UPDATE  dbo.NewOrders
SET     ShipDate = ShipDate + 1
WHERE   SalesOrderID BETWEEN 55555 AND 55557;
GO
```

```
SELECT   *
FROM     DBlocks
WHERE    spid = @@spid
         AND entity_name = 'NewOrders';
GO
ROLLBACK TRAN


-- STEP 5: Generate RangeI-N locks

-- First delete a row so that there is a gap in the
-- range for insertion
DELETE   FROM NewOrders
WHERE    SalesOrderID = 55556;

-- Now select a range of rows
BEGIN TRAN
SELECT   *
FROM     NewOrders
WHERE    SalesOrderID BETWEEN 55555 AND 55557;

--  On another connection, try to insert a row into the locked range

-- SET IDENTITY_INSERT NewOrders ON;
-- GO

-- INSERT INTO NewOrders
--            (SalesOrderID
--            ,RevisionNumber
--            ,OrderDate
--            ,DueDate
--            ,ShipDate
--            ,Status
--            ,OnlineOrderFlag
--            ,SalesOrderNumber
--            ,PurchaseOrderNumber
--            ,AccountNumber
--            ,CustomerID
--            ,ContactID
--            ,SalesPersonID
--            ,TerritoryID
--            ,BillToAddressID
--            ,ShipToAddressID
--            ,ShipMethodID
--            ,CreditCardID
```

```
--              ,CreditCardApprovalCode
--              ,CurrencyRateID
--              ,SubTotal
--              ,TaxAmt
--              ,Freight
--              ,TotalDue
--              ,Comment
--              ,rowguid
--              ,ModifiedDate
--      SELECT
--        55556,3,getdate(),getdate() +14,
--          getdate() +7 ,5 ,0 ,'SO55556',
--          'PO18444174099' ,'10-4020-000646',
--          514,99,283 ,1,876,
--          876 ,5,806,'95555Vi4081',NULL,3400,272 ,14.99,
--          3686.99 ,NULL ,newid() ,getdate()
--GO

SELECT  *
FROM    DBlocks
WHERE   entity_name = 'NewOrders';
GO

ROLLBACK TRAN
```

Listing 3-3:   Generating key-range locks.

RangeS-S
(shared key-range and shared resource lock)

When transactions are running in **SERIALIZABLE** isolation level, SQL Server will hold onto individual shared key locks on the selected data, and if an index is used to access the data, it will hold onto shared key-range locks on the intervals between index keys.

Step 2 of Listing 3-3 shows a query, running as a **SERIALIZABLE** transaction, which requests a range of orders from the **NewOrders** table, based on **SalesOrderID**, and demonstrates the acquisition of key-range S-S (**RangeS-S**) locks. The results from the

DBLocks view shows that SQL Server acquired four RangeS-S locks on KEY resources and that the SELECT statement returns three rows. It is normal to see one more key-range lock than the number of rows affected, because the ranges are open at the lower-valued end.

To understand what ranges will need to be locked, in order to prevent phantom-row insertion, we need to think about how SQL Server will try to store any newly-inserted values, and remember that a range lock prevents SQL Server from inserting a new row into the locked range.

Since the SalesOrderID column has an index, the rows will be stored in order of the SalesOrderID. The key-range locks will have to include the range from the key just prior to the first one selected up to and including the first key, so that the first key itself cannot be modified. The key-range locks will also have to include a range starting just after the highest-valued key selected up to the next key in the index, so that no values equal to the highest key selected can be inserted.

In Step 2 of Listing 3-3, the keys selected are the three consecutive values from 55555 to 55557. The four key-range locks, indicated by the four RangeS-S locks in DBLocks view, cover:

- the range starting just after the key 55554 up to and including the key 55555

- the range starting just after the key 55555 up to and including the key 55556

- the range starting just after the key 55556 up to and including the key 55557

- the range starting just after the key 55557 up to and including the key 55558.

If an index is not used to retrieve the rows, and the table is a heap, there can't be range locks, because range locks are always ranges of keys. If operating in SERIALIZABLE isolation level and no useful index is found, for the range specified in the search clause (in this case, the search clause is WHERE SalesOrderID BETWEEN 55555 and 55557), SQL Server will usually just resort to locking the entire table.

RangeS-U
(shared key-range and update resource lock)

If a non-clustered index is used to locate and update rows in a heap, while in SERIALIZABLE isolation level, and if the column being updated is *not* the indexed column used for access, the SQL Server will acquire a lock of Type RangeS-U. This means that there is an S lock on the range between the index keys, but the index key itself has a U lock. The rows in the heap will have the expected X lock on the RID. Run Step 3 in Listing 3-3 to observe these locks.

RangeX-X
(exclusive key-range and exclusive resource lock)

If updating rows in an index while in SERIALIZABLE isolation level, the session will acquire exclusive key-range locks. Step 4 in Listing 3-3, which demonstrates the acquisition of these RangeX-X locks, starts by converting the non-clustered index on SalesOrderID to a clustered index, and then updates the same range of rows as previous.

In order to observe RangeX-X locks, the updated rows must be index keys, which is true in Step 4 when the table has a clustered index, and would also occur when updating one of the key columns of a non-clustered index.

RangeI-N
(insert key-range and no resource lock)

This kind of lock indicates an exclusive lock to prevent inserts on the range between keys and no lock on the keys themselves. The lock on the range is a special type, I, which only occurs as part of a key-range lock, and since there is no existing resource to lock, the second part of the name is N (for Null).

SQL Server acquires `RangeI-N` locks when it attempts to insert values into the range between keys in `SERIALIZABLE` isolation level. We don't often see this type of lock because it is typically transient, held only until the correct location for insertion is found, and then escalated into an X lock. However, if one transaction scans a range of data using the `SERIALIZABLE` isolation level and then another transaction tries to `INSERT` into that range, the second transaction will have a lock request in a `WAIT` state, with the `RangeI-N` mode.

We can observe this behavior by running Step 5 of Listing 3-3, on two separate connections. In the original connection, we first `DELETE` a row in the range we will be scanning so that there is room for an `INSERT`. We then begin a transaction and select from a range of rows, but without committing or rolling back the transaction. Opening a new connection, we attempt to `INSERT` a new row with same key as the row that we just deleted. This insert blocks because the transaction on the first connection is still open and has the range locked. Return to the original connection, and run the query against the `DBLocks` view, to reveal that the second connection has a lock request in a `WAIT` state with the `RangeI-N` mode.

Conversion key-range locks

In addition to the four key-range lock types described in the previous sections, a few additional types, called **Conversion key-range locks**, need just a brief mention. SQL Server acquires these locks when a key-range lock overlaps another lock, as shown in Table 3-2.

If one session initially acquires the type of lock in the **Lock 1** column and then, while still holding that first lock, it acquires the lock in the **Lock 2** column, the resulting lock is the one shown in the **Conversion Lock** column.

Lock 1	Lock 2	Conversion Lock
S	Rangel-N	Rangel-S
U	Rangel-N	Rangel-U
X	Rangel-N	Rangel-X
Rangel-N	RangeS-S	RangeX-S
Rangel-N	RangeS-U	RangeX-U

Table 3-2:   Types of conversion key-range locks.

Lock Escalation

By default, SQL Server will acquire the finest-grain lock possible, in order to attain the greatest concurrency. In most cases, this means SQL Server will acquire row (`RID` or `KEY`) locks. SQL Server can acquire hundreds or thousands of individual locks on data in a single table without causing any problems. In some cases, however, if SQL Server determines that a query will access a range of rows within a clustered index, it may instead acquire page locks. After all, if every row on a page is going to be accessed, it's easier to manage a single page lock than dozens, or hundreds, of row locks. In other cases, primarily when there is no usable index to help process a query, SQL Server may lock an entire table right at the beginning of processing a query.

As we'll see in the next chapter, *Controlling Locking*, we can force SQL Server to change the default granularity of its locks with hints or index options. SQL Server can escalate locks based on total SQL Server instance resource usage, or on the number of locks acquired by one statement.

Escalation based on SQL Server instance resource usage

In some cases, acquiring individual locks on rows may end up consuming too much of SQL Server's memory. Although the memory required for each lock is quite small (about 96 bytes per lock), this still adds up to a sizeable portion of the total available memory, when thousands of locks are acquired. When SQL Server ends up using more than 24% of its buffer pool (excluding AWE memory) to keep track of locks acquired and lock requests waiting, it will choose any session holding locks and escalate its fine-grained (row or page) locks into a table lock.

Alternatively, we can specify that we want server-wide lock escalation to be triggered based on the total number of locks held by all sessions on the instance. If we change the value of the LOCKS configuration option to something other than the default value of zero, SQL Server will start choosing sessions to have their locks escalated as soon as it has acquired 40% of that configured total number of locks. For example, if we configure LOCKS to be 10,000, then escalation will start as soon as there are 4,000 locks held or requested.

When the instance-wide escalation is triggered by crossing the memory threshold or by acquiring too many locks, we have no control over which sessions will have their locks escalated to table locks, and should just consider it a random selection.

In addition, as long as the memory use remains over the instance-wide threshold, for every 1,250 new locks, SQL Server will again start escalating fine-grained locks into table locks.

Escalation based on number of locks held by a single statement

In addition to escalating locks when an instance-wide threshold is crossed, SQL Server will also escalate locks when any individual session acquires more than 5,000 locks in a single statement. In this case, there is no randomness in choosing which session will get its locks escalated; it is the session that acquired the locks.

Listing 3-4 demonstrates this escalation behavior in the **AdventureWorks** database. First, we start a transaction and perform two **UPDATE** statements. Together, the two statements acquire more than 5,000 locks, but neither one, individually, acquires that many. Lock escalation does not occur, and the **DBLocks** query should reveal that the number of X locks held by the connection is 6,342.

In the second transaction, we update the same 6,342 rows in a single statement. In this case, the **DBLocks** query reveals that the total number of locks held, right before the end of the transaction, is only one (a table lock).

```
USE AdventureWorks;

-- First show that if no one statement gets more than 5000 locks
-- there will be no escalation
BEGIN TRAN
UPDATE   Sales.SalesOrderHeader
SET      DueDate = DueDate + 1
WHERE    salesOrderID < 46000;


UPDATE   Sales.SalesOrderHeader
SET      DueDate = DueDate + 1
WHERE    salesOrderID BETWEEN 46000 AND 50000;


SELECT   *
FROM     DBLocks
WHERE    mode = 'X'
         AND spid = @@spid;
-- 6342 total locks
ROLLBACK TRAN;
GO
BEGIN TRAN
-- Now show that if the same total number of locks are acquired in a
-- single statement, we will get escalation and the sys.dm_tran_locks
-- query will only show 1 lock
UPDATE   Sales.SalesOrderHeader
SET      DueDate = DueDate + 1
WHERE    salesOrderID <= 50000;


SELECT   *
FROM     DBLocks
WHERE    mode = 'X'
         AND spid = @@spid;
-- 1 lock
ROLLBACK TRAN;
GO
```

Listing 3-4:   Lock escalation based on number of rows.

Other Types of Locks

The types of lock discussed previously in this chapter and in Chapter 2, represent the types of locks we'll encounter most frequently when investigating locking and blocking activity in SQL Server. However, two other types of locks can sometimes cause unexpected blocking problems, so we must cover them briefly.

Latches

Latches are similar to locks, but they are applied at the physical level, and are not as "expensive" to maintain and manage as locks, because latches use fewer system resources and their duration is usually quite short. Latches and locks seem very similar because both of them can show up as the `last_wait_type` column in the `sys.dm_exec_requests` view, which we'll discuss in Chapter 5, on troubleshooting concurrency problems. SQL Trace and Windows Performance Monitor have dozens of counters for monitoring latches, which look very similar to the counters for monitoring locks. Like locks, latches can be shared or exclusive, and can be granted or in a wait state.

However, latches do not show up in the `sys.dm_tran_locks` view. Latches are used to protect an internal structure for brief periods while it is being read or modified, not to ensure correct transaction behavior. Both the data page itself and the buffer that the data is occupying are protected by latches.

Another way of considering the difference between a lock and a latch is that a lock is something *we* need to protect data integrity, for example to make sure that another transaction does not update data that your transaction is examining; there is nothing inside SQL Server to prevent this kind of change. SQL Server doesn't "care" if another transaction changes data your transaction is examining, so we need to use the proper isolation level and transaction control mechanisms to make sure the data is locked appropriately. On the other hand, latches are something that *SQL Server* needs, to protect the physical structure of the data. If a session were to try to update a page while SQL Server was reading or writing that page to disk, the page could become corrupted. Latches prevent this kind of violation of the data. Latches protect the *physical* integrity of the data; locks protect its *logical* integrity.

We can exert very little influence on how and when SQL Server acquires or holds latches, and usually they are so transient as to be barely noticeable. Typically, SQL Server will acquire a latch while it is reading data pages into cache but, as soon as the pages are read, locks are acquired and the latch is released. Latches are not transaction based, which is one of the factors that makes them so transient.

Latching is very rarely a cause for concern but you may come across Errors 844 and 845, which both indicate that a timeout occurred while waiting for a latch on a buffer. These errors are almost always caused by problems at the hardware level, including suboptimal I/O systems incapable of meeting the demand being placed on them, misconfiguration of the SQL Server system, or bad index design, leading to SQL Server having to perform many times more read operations than is necessary.

Compile locks

In SQL Server 2008, only one copy of a compiled stored procedure plan is generally in cache at any given time. In order to make sure there aren't multiple copies, certain parts of the SQL Server compilation process must be serialized so that only one session at a time can be compiling a particular routine. This discussion is also relevant to triggers and some types of user-defined functions.

Compile locks are acquired during the parts of the compilation process that must be serialized. Usually SQL Server holds the locks for a very short period but, in some cases, when many sessions are trying to execute the same procedure simultaneously, and if the procedure is not schema-qualified when called, we may end up with noticeable concurrency problems due to compile locks.

Although SQL Server needs to take compile locks any time it needs to recompile a procedure, if it needs to recompile a procedure *every time* it runs, the situation is much worse, and this will happen when users execute a procedure without qualifying the procedure with the schema name.

For example, assume we have a stored procedure called `MyProc` that is stored in the `dbo` schema, but is executed by a user, Sue, who has a default schema of `sue_schema`. If Sue invokes the procedure with `EXEC MyProc`, SQL Server will, on the first execution, fail to find the object in cache. Even if there is a plan for `MyProc` in cache, SQL Server does not know this is the right plan to use unless it can verify whether there is another routine called `MyProc` in `sue_schema`. SQL Server acquires an exclusive compile lock on the procedure and prepares to compile the procedure, which would include resolving the object name to an object ID. Once SQL Server has this object ID, it can then definitely determine whether there really is a valid plan for the requested procedure. If there is a usable plan in cache, SQL Server can use that plan and does not actually need to compile the requested procedure. However, because of the lack of schema-qualification, SQL Server had to perform a second cache lookup and acquire an exclusive compile lock before determining that it could reuse the existing cached execution plan.

Acquiring the lock and performing the necessary system table lookups can introduce a delay that is sufficient for the compile locks to lead to blocking. While the duration of the blocking is usually not very long, per session, if there are many sessions invoking the same procedure, without owner-qualifying it, then as soon as one compilation finishes, another session takes over the role of head blocker for a few seconds or less, and so forth, causing a situation called *rolling blocking*.

In the `sys.dm_exec_requests` DMV, these compile locks can be identified by the occurrence of a blocked session with a `last_wait_type` value of `LCK_M_X` (indicating an X lock, and the string `[[COMPILE]]` appearing after the resource ID. The blocker session may also show `LCK_M_X` as its `last_wait_type`, but it will have a status of `RUNNABLE` whereas the blocked session will have a status of `SLEEPING`.

The `wait_resource` value will look as if it is referencing a table because it will show the keyword TAB, but the object ID reported is actually the object ID of a routine (a procedure, a trigger, or a function).

Fortunately, this type of blocking has a very easy fix; if you always schema qualify your stored procedure names, this problem is greatly reduced.

Non-Lock-Related Causes of Blocking

As noted earlier, by far the most common type of resource for which a session may have to wait is a lock. However, SQL Server must also wait for memory resources to be available for certain kinds of queries, especially queries requiring hashing or sorting which require special worktables during execution. In some cases, SQL Server may have to wait for network resources to be available, especially when executing queries on a linked server. Since SQL Server guarantees that it will write to the transaction log on disk the log records for all committed transactions, a session that has just finished a transaction may need to wait if the log reader is not fast enough, or disk writing is too slow.

Later, in Chapter 5, we'll discuss some of the types of waits indicated in the `sys.dm_exec_requests` view in more detail, and encounter a few more types of resources that may cause a session to have to wait.

Summary

In this chapter, we looked some more advanced locking topics, including lock mode conversion, when SQL Server acquires additional locks on data that is already locked. We covered the special lock mode called key-range locks that can be held on ranges of index keys when running queries under SERIALIZABLE isolation level. We looked at when, and how, SQL Server will escalate locks on smaller resources into table or partition locks. Finally, we explored latches and compile locks.

Chapter 4: Controlling Locking

As has been noted throughout this book, it is best, wherever possible, to let SQL Server decide on the locking strategies that work best with our applications. As long as these applications are designed well, the locks acquired by default will be the ones necessary to safeguard data integrity during concurrent access, according to the established transaction isolation level, and will rarely cause severe blocking.

Of course, not all applications have an "ideal" design, and SQL Server doesn't always make the right choices, so in rare cases we may need to override SQL Server's default locking behavior. Generally, this will be because the application behavior leads us to doubt that SQL Server made the right choice, so we want to force SQL Server to do something different, just to see what happens. In many such situations, it will turn out that SQL Server actually did make the best choice, but there may be times where the forced behavior is optimal.

In this chapter, we discuss several different mechanisms for changing the way that SQL Server acquires and manages locks.

- Changing the transaction isolation level (the most common method).

- Changing the lock timeout period so that a transaction either skips past the locked rows, or rolls back.

- Using lock hints in SQL statements to control lock granularity, or specify custom behavior on encountering locked rows.

- Using bound connections to allow multiple connections to share the same locks.

- Using application locks to extend the resources that can be locked.

Controlling Concurrency and Locking Via the Isolation Level

We discussed isolation levels in detail in Chapter 1, along with code examples that explored the SET options for controlling the isolation level. Here, we'll review the implications of each level in terms of the locking strategy implemented by SQL Server. We set the isolation level for the current connection with the following command:

```
SET TRANSACTION ISOLATION LEVEL <level_specifier>
Where the <level_specifier> can be one of the five values below.
```

- **READ UNCOMMITTED** – A transaction operating in READ UNCOMMITTED isolation level takes no locks while performing SELECT operations so it cannot block on locks held by other transactions.

- **READ COMMITTED** – The default isolation level, in which SQL Server holds shared locks only until the data has been read, and holds exclusive locks until the end of the transaction.

- **REPEATABLE READ** – A transaction operating in REPEATABLE READ isolation level keeps shared locks and exclusive locks until the end of the transaction.

- **SERIALIZABLE** – The most restrictive isolation level, SERIALIZABLE adopts a special locking mechanism, using key-range locks, and holds all locks until the end of the transaction, so that users can't insert new rows into those ranges.

- **SNAPSHOT** – Has the outward appearance of SERIALIZABLE, but operates under a completely different concurrency model, optimistic concurrency, which we'll be discussing in Chapter 6.

Remember that increasing the transaction isolation level comes at a cost. Although we can guarantee predictable behavior by keeping data locked for the duration of the transaction, other transactions will block and system throughput can decrease.

The big downside of choosing the less restrictive READ UNCOMMITTED level, to remove locking, is the possibility of reading data that has not yet been committed, and that might, therefore, later be rolled back by a transaction. However, this is far from the only problem that can occur when using the READ UNCOMMITTED isolation level. When using it, SQL Server takes no locks during SELECT operations so, if one session is scanning a table while another is updating it, the scanning session might end up reading the same row twice, or it might completely miss some rows. It is even possible to get incorrect results when performing table aggregates under READ UNCOMMITTED isolation.

Many people choose READ UNCOMMITTED to get faster response times, as will happen when SQL Server doesn't have to wait for a lock, but the tradeoff is frequently correctness. Do we want our data fast and possibly incorrect, or correct but possibly slower?

All SET options, including those for changing the transaction isolation level, remain in effect for the entire session and apply to all batches and transactions executed in that session. To control locking at a more granular level, we can use a locking hint to apply any of the transaction isolation levels to any or all tables in a query. We'll discuss locking hints shortly.

Setting a Lock Timeout

By default, SQL Server operates as though any session will eventually release any locked data and will continue to wait until it is, regardless of how long that might be. There may be times when, for certain connections, we wish to limit the length of time SQL Server should wait for a session to release a lock. This may happen in a system in which there are multiple reports or processing operations, but no particular sequence in which they must execute. If one of the activities is blocked, we may just choose to have SQL Server proceed to the next one.

In SQL Server 6.5 and earlier versions, there was no way to tell SQL Server to stop waiting for a lock. There was an option to set a connection timeout setting through many client interfaces and tools, including ODBC and the ISQL/W tool (a precursor to SQL Server Management Studio), but a connection timeout setting merely tells the client to cancel the query, if SQL Server hasn't returned results in a specified amount of time. The client doesn't know *why* the results haven't come back. The cause might be a lock, or network problems, or it might be a long-running query that takes more than the set value to finish executing.

The option SET LOCK_TIMEOUT tells SQL Server not to wait more than a specified number of milliseconds for a session to release a lock. Setting LOCK_TIMEOUT to zero means that SQL Server won't wait at all if it finds any locked data. Setting LOCK_ TIMEOUT to –1 returns it to the default behavior of waiting indefinitely. We can check the current value by examining the parameterless function @@lock_timeout.

The LOCK_TIMEOUT setting might sound like just what you've been waiting for, but use it with extreme caution. If a session stays blocked for longer than the LOCK_TIMEOUT setting, SQL Server generates a lock timeout error. This error doesn't automatically roll back a transaction. Therefore, when SQL Server reaches its lock timeout value, it stops trying to modify rows in the current table and moves on to the next statement. Instead of the transaction being an atomic, all-or-nothing operation, we might be left with part of the transaction incompletely executed.

If the required behavior is that specific queries don't wait at all on encountering a lock, an alternative to the LOCK_TIMEOUT setting, which applies to the entire session, is to use the NOWAIT hint. This hint sets a lock timeout of 0 for a single table in a single statement. We'll take a look at an example of the LOCK_TIMEOUT setting in action in the next section, where we compare its behavior to some hints.

If the transaction must be all or nothing, we can add **TRY/CATCH** error handling and include a specific test for Error 1222, which would then perform a **ROLLBACK TRANS-ACTION** on encountering the error. Alternatively, we could use the **SET** option **SET XACT_ABORT ON**, which instructs SQL Server to roll back the transaction any time any error occurs. This means that if Error 1222 occurs, SQL Server will roll back the transaction automatically. However, bear in mind that any other error, such as trying to insert a duplicate value into a unique index, will also cause the entire transaction to roll back. This might not always be what we want.

Locking Hints

Locking hints in SQL Server fall into the general category of table hints, because they are specified in the **FROM** clause, after the name of the table to which they should be applied. Table hints apply to one table; if we want to apply the same hint to all tables, we must specify the hint after each table name. There is no way for a single hint to control locking behavior on every table in a query. To change the locking behavior on all tables, for a specified session, we must change the isolation level setting.

The problem with the term "hint" is that it makes it sound like merely a suggestion. However, except in cases where the hint makes no sense and is ignored, and a very few cases where an error message is generated because a non-existent object was referenced, a hint acts more like a directive; SQL Server *will* use the locking strategy specified by that hint.

The SQL Server 2008 documentation lists 15 table hints that control locking or SQL Server's response to locked data.

HOLDLOCK	NOLOCK	NOWAIT	PAGLOCK
READCOMMITTED	READCOMMITTEDLOCK	READPAST	READUNCOMMITTED
REPEATABLEREAD	ROWLOCK	SERIALIZABLE	TABLOCK
TABLOCKX	UPDLOCK	XLOCK	

The HOLDLOCK hint is available for backward compatibility only and is equivalent to the SERIALIZABLE hint. NOLOCK is equivalent to the preferred hint, READUNCOMMITTED. The four hints READUNCOMMITTED, READCOMMITTED, REPEATABLEREAD, and SERIALIZABLE mimic the behavior of the four ANSI isolation levels, but apply only to one table in one query. Four hints control the unit of locking: ROWLOCK, PAGLOCK, TABLOCK, and TABLOCKX.

The UPDLOCK and XLOCK hints control the type of lock, but not the unit of locking. We saw UPDLOCK in the last chapter when illustrating special intent locks, and we'll see it again in the next chapter as a way to help avoid conflicts under SNAPSHOT isolation. The XLOCK hint can help ensure that no other connection can access the locked resource, and that SQL Server holds the lock until the end of the transaction.

The READPAST hint is a special kind of hint; it doesn't control the type of lock or the unit of locking, but instead lets a transaction skip locked rows, rather than be blocked. If one connection has one or more rows locked, then if a transaction in another connection, running with the READPAST hint, attempts to read the locked data, if will ignore any locked rows and move to the next unlocked row. If the "blocking" connection holds page locks, or a table lock, then SQL Server ignores the READPAST hint and the second connection will be blocked. This hint can be useful in a work queue where a clerk needs to retrieve an order to process, but it doesn't matter exactly which one. The READPAST hint allows SQL Server to retrieve the first unlocked row it finds.

The NOLOCK and READPAST hints, as well as the SET LOCK_TIMEOUT setting, allow us to specify what SQL Server does when it finds itself blocked from accessing the data it needs. It is important to understand the differences between these three options, and the code in Listing 4-1 compares them.

```
-- Three ways to get around locked data
-- Make sure all existing connections are closed first
-- Open a new connection and execute the following batch:

--   Connection 1:
USE AdventureWorks;
SELECT   SalesOrderID ,
         DueDate ,
         CustomerID ,
         TotalDue
FROM     Sales.SalesOrderHeader
WHERE    CustomerID = 26;
GO


-- This will show you the 3 rows in the SalesOrderHeader table
-- with the CustomerID value of 26

-- Now in the same connection, execute this batch:
BEGIN TRAN
UPDATE   Sales.SalesOrderHeader
SET      DueDate = '1/1/2200'
WHERE    SalesOrderID = 45578;
GO

-- Do not terminate this transaction!
------------------------------------------------------
-- On another connection, execute the following:
-- Connection 2
USE AdventureWorks;
SELECT   SalesOrderID ,
         DueDate ,
         CustomerID ,
         TotalDue
FROM     Sales.SalesOrderHeader WITH ( NOLOCK )
WHERE    CustomerID = 26;
GO

-- Note that with the NOLOCK hint, you'll see the new
-- much later date, even though the change
-- hasn't been committed


------------------------------------------------------------
```

```
-- On another connection, execute the following:
-- Connection 3

USE AdventureWorks;
SELECT  SalesOrderID ,
        DueDate ,
        CustomerID ,
        TotalDue
FROM    Sales.SalesOrderHeader WITH ( READPAST )
WHERE   CustomerID = 26
GO
-- Note that with the READPAST hint, we will skip over
-- the one locked row, only see two rows returned


--------------------------------------------------------
-- On another connection, execute the following:
-- Connection 4
USE AdventureWorks;
SET LOCK_TIMEOUT 5000;
GO
SELECT  *
FROM    Sales.SalesOrderHeader
WHERE   CustomerID = 26;
GO

-- The lock timeout has been set to 5 seconds. This
-- batch will wait 5 seconds and then return error 1222.
-- It will never return any rows.


-- Return to Connection 1:
ROLLBACK TRANSACTION;
GO
```

Listing 4-1: Controlling the effects of locking using lock hints and a lock timeout.

Sharing Locks Across Connections

So far in this chapter we've considered several ways in which, for a given session, table, or connection, a user can opt to allow a transaction to continue reading data regardless of what locks other transactions many hold on that data. We can set the isolation level to READ UNCOMMITTED, or use the NOLOCK hint, to read whatever data value currently exists, even if it's uncommitted; or we can use the READPAST hint, or SET LOCK_TIMEOUT, to "skip past" locked rows (or to roll back on encountering locked rows, in the latter case). In such cases, the lock-holding session has no say in whether or not other sessions can have access to its locked data; the requesting session simply demands access to the data, "no matter what."

Occasionally, however, it is useful to have the holding session issue an "entry pass" that will let only certain other sessions, such as those arising from the same application, access the data it has locked. This is the basic idea behind the "bound connections" feature. Bound connections allow sessions to share locks and help prevent a situation called "application deadlock," which is described in the following paragraphs.

A SQL Server session that is holding locks on a resource does not lock itself from the resource; only other sessions are denied access. However, if a single application process actually initiates two separate sessions in SQL Server to perform its work, then SQL Server will treat them as two completely separate processes; if one of them requests a lock that is incompatible with locks already held by the other, then blocking will occur.

In fact, it's possible to encounter a situation called an "application deadlock," which is not detected by SQL Server as a deadlock. An application opens one connection and starts reading data, retrieving it from SQL Server one row at a time. When it finds a row of interest, it uses another connection to submit an UPDATE request to SQL Server. The UPDATE is likely to block, because the first connection's SQL Server session may still be holding a shared lock on the row.

SQL Server will not release the shared lock until the application moves on and reads more rows through the first connection. However, the application *cannot* move on until the UPDATE in the second connection completes. Therefore, at the application layer, the first connection is waiting for the second to complete its work; at the SQL Server layer, the second session with the UPDATE is waiting for the lock held by the first session, reading the data.

SQL Server will not detect the preceding situation as deadlock, because it is only aware of what is going on at the SQL Server layer, not at the application layer, which is managing the two connections.

One solution is to allow two or more different connections to share a lock space, by request, and so not lock each other out; by default, no sharing of the "lock space" occurs between connections, even if they belong to the same user and the same application. This capability is known as **bound connections**. With bound connections, the first connection asks SQL Server to give out a bind token, which it passes to the application (using a client-side global variable, shared memory, or another method) for use in subsequent connections. The bind token acts as a "magic cookie" so that other connections can share the lock space of the original connection blocking any connection to which it is bound. These bind tokens are managed by using the two system stored procedures `sp_getbindtoken` and `sp_bindsession`.

In older versions of SQL Server, bound connections were especially useful when writing an extended stored procedure (a function written in your own DLL) that needed to call back into the database to do some work. Without a bound connection, the extended stored procedure could collide with the locks of its own calling process. In more recent versions of SQL Server, stored procedures written using CLR are more secure, scalable, and stable than extended stored procedures. CLR-stored procedures use the `SqlContext` object to join the context of the calling session, not `sp_bindsession`.

We can use bound connections to develop multi-tier applications in which two separate programs must perform work as a single business operation in a single transaction. When using bound connections, the sessions used by each program will share the same locks and so we must write the programs involved carefully to coordinate their access to the data, and avoid trying to modify the same data at the same time.

When multiple processes share a lock space and a transaction space by using bound connections, a COMMIT or ROLLBACK affects all the participating connections. However, each session has its own isolation level, and using SET TRANSACTION ISOLATION LEVEL in one session does not affect the isolation level of any other session bound to it.

Bound connections in action

Listing 4-2 shows an example of creating bound connections between two different connections in SQL Server Management Studio. A bind token can only be acquired inside an explicit transaction. Since we don't have a controlling application to declare and store the bind token in an application variable, we have to actually copy it from one query window and paste it into a second.

```
-- Make sure all existing connections are closed first
-- Open a new connection and execute the following batch:

-- Connection 1:
USE AdventureWorks;
DECLARE @token VARCHAR(255);
BEGIN TRAN
EXEC sp_getbindtoken @token OUTPUT;
SELECT  @token;
GO

-- This should return something like the following:
--     -----------dPe---5---.?jOU<_WP?1HMK-3/D8;@

-- Use your mouse to select the complete token
-- string that was returned from the last SELECT statement.
```

```
-- Open a second Query window, and execute the
-- following: (Be sure and paste in whatever bind token
-- string you received; do not just use the one printed
-- here.)

-- Connection 2:
EXEC sp_bindsession 'dPe---5---.?j0U<_WP?1HMK-3/D8;@1';
GO
```

Listing 4-2:   Creating bound connections.

Normally, we wouldn't have to look at the messy token string; the application would just store it and pass it on. However, for this quick example using a query window, it's necessary to see the value.

Once the **sp_bindsession** is executed in the second window, the two sessions are bound together. Any data locked in the first session is accessible by the second; a transaction started by the first can be rolled back by the second.

Listing 4-3 is the continuation of Listing 4-2 and shows that we can now go back to the first query window and execute a command that locks some data. Remember that we have already begun a transaction in order to call **sp_getbindtoken**.

```
-- Go back to the first query window, where we are already
-- in a transaction

-- Connection 1:
-- Execute the following batch:

UPDATE   Sales.SalesOrderHeader
SET      DueDate = '1/1/2200'
WHERE    CustomerID = 26;
GO

-- This should exclusively lock every row in the table for CustomerID 26
-- Now go to the second query window and select from the locked table:
```

```
-- Execute this batch in the second query window:

-- Connection 2:
SELECT  *
FROM    Sales.SalesOrderHeader
WHERE   CustomerID = 26;
GO
ROLLBACK TRAN;
GO

-- Return to the original query window, where you
-- started the transaction, and attempt to execute:

-- Connection 1:
ROLLBACK TRANSACTION;
GO

-- You should get an error message saying there is no
-- corresponding BEGIN TRANSACTION statement.
```

Listing 4-3:   Observing the behavior of bound connections.

In the second query window, we should be able to see future DueDate values, just as if it were part of the same connection performing the UPDATE. Besides sharing lock space, the bound connections also share transaction space. When we execute a ROLLBACK TRAN in the second session, we cannot then roll back the transaction in the first session. If we issued a ROLLBACK TRAN in the first session, we would see the message below.

```
The transaction active in this session has been committed or aborted by another
session
Server: Msg 3903, Level 16, State 1, Line 1
The ROLLBACK TRANSACTION request has no corresponding BEGIN TRANSACTION
The transaction active in this session has been committed or aborted by another
session.
```

Bound connection metadata

SQL Server keeps track of bound connections in the system view **sys.dm_tran_session_transactions**. If the code in Listing 4-4 is run before any **ROLLBACK** operations, in either of the connections involved in our bound sessions, we should get results similar to those shown in Figure 4-1. We can see that two different sessions share the same **transaction_id** value. The session with the **is_local** value of 1 is the initiating session, and the one with the **is_bound** value of 1 is the session that bound itself to the initiator.

```
SELECT   session_id ,
         transaction_id ,
         is_local ,
         is_bound
FROM     sys.dm_tran_session_transactions
GO
```

Listing 4-4:   Query to provide information about open transactions.

	session_id	transaction_id	is_local	is_bound
1	51	62060	1	0
2	56	62060	0	1

Figure 4-1:   Results in **sys.dm_tran_ssession_transactions** showing 51 and 56 as bound connections.

User-Defined Locks

The method used by SQL Server to store information about locking, and to check for incompatible locks, is very straightforward and extensible. Remember that the SQL Server lock manager knows nothing about the object it is locking. It works only with strings representing the resource, without knowing the actual structure of that resource. If two sessions are trying to obtain incompatible locks on the same resource, blocking will occur.

If the SQL Server engineers were to decide to allow us to lock individual columns as well as rows, pages, and tables, they could simply decide on an internal code number for column locks, and then we could add that to the list of resources visible in the `resource_type` column in `sys.dm_tran_locks`.

However, instead of adding new lock resources, SQL Server lets us extend the resources that can be locked, using **application locks**. To define an application lock, we specify a name for the resource to be locked, a mode, an owner, and a timeout. We can take advantage of the supplied mechanisms for detecting blocking situations, and we can choose to lock anything we like.

Two resources are considered to be the same resource, and are subject to blocking, if they have the same name and the same owner in the same database. Remember that by "lock owner" we mean the session, the transaction, or the cursor. For a user-defined application lock, the only possible owners are a transaction or a session. SQL Server can grant two requests for locks on the same resource if the modes of the locks requested are compatible. SQL Server checks the locks for compatibility using the same compatibility matrix used for SQL Server supplied locks.

For example, suppose we have a stored procedure, `MySpecialProc`, which only one user at a time should execute. By incorporating an application lock into `MySpecialProc`, we can ensure that, when a session is using that procedure, it is "locked," and any other session requesting to execute it will be blocked. The application lock is acquired by calling the `sp_getapplock` system stored procedure, which will be the first action performed by `MySpecialProc`. When the procedure has finished executing, we can use `sp_releaseapplock` to release the lock. Until this happens, or until the session terminates, no other session can execute this procedure as long as every session follows the protocol and uses `sp_getapplock` to request rights to the procedure before trying to execute it.

Listing 4-5 demonstrates how a procedure could incorporate an application lock to ensure that only one session at a time can execute it.

```
USE AdventureWorks;
GO
CREATE PROC MySpecialProc
AS
    DECLARE @err AS INT;
    EXEC @err = sp_getapplock 'ProcLock', 'Exclusive', 'session', 0;
    IF @err <> 0
        BEGIN
            RAISERROR('Could not acquire lock on MySpecialProc.', 16, 1);
            RETURN @err;
        END;

    PRINT 'MySpecialProc is running...';
-- Body of procedure would go here
-- The WAITFOR simulates the procedure execution and allows you
-- to observe the APPLICATION lock from another connection
    WAITFOR DELAY '00:00:10';
    EXEC sp_releaseapplock 'ProcLock', 'session';
    RETURN;
GO
```

Listing 4-5:   Creating a procedure that uses an application lock.

SQL Server doesn't know what the resource ProcLock means. It just adds a row to the sys.dm_tran_locks view, which is used to compare against other requested locks. An application lock, when we query sys.dm_tran_locks, will have a resource_type value of APPLICATION.

The resource name used in these procedures can be any identifier up to 255 characters long. However, only the first 32 characters will be visible when examining locks in sys. dm_tran_locks. The possible modes of the lock, which is used to check compatibility with other requests for this same resource, are shared, update, exclusive, intent exclusive, and intent shared. There is no default; we must specify a mode. The possible values for lock owner, the third parameter, are transaction (the default) or session. SQL Server must acquire a lock with an owner of TRANSACTION within a user-defined transaction, and will automatically release it at the end of the transaction without any need to call sp_releaseapplock. SQL Server will release a lock with an owner of SESSION automatically only when the session disconnects.

Summary

In this chapter, we looked at various techniques you can use to control SQL Server's locking behavior, for special cases where the default behavior is less than ideal. We looked at a session setting to control a lock timeout period and then looked at various locking hints that control locking for a single table in a single statement. We explored a technique that allows two connections to share the same locks, which can help the problem of application deadlock. Finally, we saw an example of a technique that allows us to create our own "application locks," in cases where we need to control access to certain operations within our applications.

Chapter 5: Troubleshooting Pessimistic Concurrency

Although troubleshooting techniques haven't been our prime focus until now, we've already seen the number one troubleshooting tool when faced with locking and blocking, namely the `sys.dm_tran_locks` DMV. We've also used my `DBLocks` view, built on top of `sys.dm_tran_locks`, which provides a custom subset of the information that is most often useful when dealing with these problems.

In this chapter, we'll take a much deeper look at troubleshooting techniques for the locking and blocking issues that occur most often when working under the pessimistic concurrency model. In doing so, we'll be using the available metadata from `sys.dm_tran_locks` as well as several other tools.

As discussed in Chapter 1, each of the three commonly used, ANSI-standard, isolation levels (`READ COMMITTED`, `REPEATABLE READ` and `SERIALIZABLE`) are implemented by SQL Server in a pessimistic fashion. In other words, SQL Server controls access to a shared resource by acquiring locks on that resource, which ensure that readers of the resource block writers and writers block readers (as well as other writers). In most cases, locking will cause no problems but there are times, when user connections appear to "hang" and business processes that normally take seconds to execute are suddenly taking minutes or more. This is when we need to leap into action and investigate possible concurrency issues, such as:

- **excessive locking** – an excessive number of locks can lead to memory-related issues and often leads to lock escalation

- **blocking** – if sessions are blocked for extended periods of time it can lead to frustratingly slow query execution times

- **deadlocking** – one session is waiting for a second session to release a resource, and vice versa. Neither can proceed.

We'll discuss how to investigate and resolve each of these issues in this chapter. In the next chapter, we'll move on to consider the optimistic concurrency model, along with concurrency issues that are most associated with that model, namely contention on the tempdb database, and update conflicts.

Troubleshooting Locking

SQL Server locks resources to ensure the logical consistency of the database, during concurrent access of those shared database resources. Locking in SQL Server does not *physically* affect a data resource such as a row, page, table, or index: it is more like a reservation system that all tasks respect when they want access to some resource within the database. Excessive numbers of locks, or locks of very long duration, can lead to blocking and other problems, and we'll discuss these issues later in the chapter. However, in cases where session activity forces SQL Server to acquire and manage a high number of locks, this in itself can present some issues. Tracking the details of each lock request, whether in a **GRANT** or a **WAIT** state, requires memory; too many locks can mean SQL Server needs too much memory just for locking. Alternatively, as we saw in Chapter 3, SQL Server can choose to escalate multiple smaller grained locks to a table lock.

Detecting lock escalation

Chapter 3 described lock escalation, and the conditions under which it can occur, either because an instance-wide "lock memory" or "lock number" threshold is passed, or because a single statement acquires more than the maximum permitted number of locks.

Often, SQL Server will lock individual rows in a table, and this is especially true if updates and deletes affect a smaller number of rows. However, there are times, such as when performing mass updates, when SQL Server may choose to escalate row locks or page locks to a single table lock, in order to achieve a more optimal use of lock memory resources.

If a whole table is locked, rather than just individual rows, then this may cause blocking and reduce concurrency, so we need a way to detect it when it occurs, and take remedial action. There are a couple of ways to detect lock escalation. The easiest way is to use the `Lock:Escalation` event class in SQL Trace/Profiler. When lock escalation occurs, the event will fire. However, a single lock escalation event in the database, on a particular table, may cause the `Lock:Escalation` trace event to fire multiple times, so it's important to be able to relate multiple rows in the trace file to the same lock escalation event. Therefore, in addition to the default columns for the `Lock:Escalation` event class, which provide the basic information, it is also useful to include in the trace columns such as `TransactionID`, `DatabaseID`, `DatabaseName`, and `ObjectID`, in order to be able to tie each row in the trace to a particular `TransactionID` and to a particular object (that is, a table).

We can use the `sys.dm_tran_locks` view to detect table locks at a given point in time and so, by inference, decide whether lock escalation may be occurring, prior to a full investigation with Profiler. For example, if we expect that an application would rarely require a shared or exclusive lock on a table, then the presence of these locks implies lock escalation. Listing 5-1 shows an example.

```
SELECT   request_session_id ,
         resource_type ,
         DB_NAME(resource_database_id) AS DatabaseName ,
         OBJECT_NAME(resource_associated_entity_id) AS TableName ,
         request_mode ,
         request_type ,
         request_status
FROM     sys.dm_tran_locks AS L
         JOIN sys.all_objects AS A ON L.resource_associated_entity_id = A.object_id
WHERE    request_type = 'LOCK'
         AND request_status = 'GRANT'
         AND request_mode IN ( 'X', 'S' )
         AND A.type = 'U'
         AND resource_type = 'OBJECT'
         AND L.resource_database_id = DB_ID();
```

Listing 5-1: Query to detect non-intent table locks.

Listing 5-1 references the `sys.all_objects` catalog view, so the information returned is scoped to the target database for the query. The `sys.dm_tran_locks` view does not return details about the object locked, so it offers no way to tell directly whether the object is actually a table. Consequently, we have to join with something in the database that will return that information, and in this case `sys.all_objects` contains the object type (`'U'` indicates a user table), and the `OBJECT_NAME` function can return the name of the table. However, both the `sys.all_objects` view and the `OBJECT_NAME` function will only return information from the current database. For this reason, the last condition in the query restricts the returned rows to those resources in the current database.

Resolving lock escalation

If escalation has actually caused blocking problems, the best solution is usually to try to tune queries, ensuring that appropriate indexes are used and as few pages as possible need to be accessed, and as few locks as possible need to be acquired. In addition, a best practice is always to keep transactions as short as possible, so that SQL Server doesn't acquire and hold any non-essential locks.

In addition, it is a best practice to reduce the batch sizes of mass inserts, updates, or deletes such that we prevent unwanted lock escalation. For a mass update, for example, we can limit each batch to a certain number of rows, or to a maximum of 5,000 locks. It's important to test this to try to find the maximum number of rows-per-batch that will prevent escalation. SQL Server can detect that a query will be iterating through the table and may escalate the locks anyway.

Controlling escalation

There are occasions where we may wish to prevent escalation altogether, for a certain table. If the table must be available at all times by as many sessions as possible, because of key lookup data it contains, it can impact an entire application if one session is able to lock the entire table.

Using ALTER TABLE SET LOCK_ESCALATION (SQL Server 2008 and later)

Locks never escalate from row to page, but they can escalate from row to table or from page to table. As of SQL Server 2008, locks can also escalate to a partition, or we can disable escalation for a table, but only if we use the ALTER TABLE SET LOCK_ESCALATION option:

```
ALTER TABLE <table_name> SET (LOCK_ESCALATION = [TABLE | AUTO | DISABLE);
```

The three possible values for the LOCK_ESCALATION option, specified after the name of the table, are shown below.

- **TABLE** – The default value, indicating that when one of the escalation thresholds described previously is crossed, and this table is chosen for escalation, the escalation will be to lock the entire table.

- **AUTO** – This indicates that if the table is partitioned, and a single statement updates more than 5,000 rows in a single partition, the row locks will be escalated to a partition lock. Once SQL Server has acquired partition locks, it will never escalate to table locks.

- **DISABLE** – This disallows escalation for this table, no matter how many locks SQL Server acquires. Note that this does not mean that SQL Server will never acquire table-level locks for this table. In some cases, SQL Server will acquire table locks as query processing starts and this is not considered escalation. Be careful when disabling escalation for a huge table, as this would mean SQL Server is forced to keep potentially tens of thousands (or more!) page locks, which will require a substantial amount of memory.

Using intent locks

Pre-SQL Server 2008, there is still a trick we can use to prevent escalation on a single table, and that is to force SQL Server to acquire an intent lock without actually locking any rows.

Once one transaction has an intent lock, another transaction cannot escalate its locks to a table lock. For example, suppose we want to prevent lock escalation on the Sales.SalesOrderDetail table in the sample database AdventureWorks2008. The query in Listing 5-2 will prevent lock escalation on the Sales.SalesOrderDetail table for one hour.

```
BEGIN TRAN
SELECT  *
FROM    Sales.SalesOrderDetail WITH ( UPDLOCK, HOLDLOCK )
WHERE   1 = 0;
WAITFOR DELAY '1:00:00'
COMMIT
```

Listing 5-2:   Forcing SQL Server to acquire an intent lock to prevent lock escalation.

In SQL Profiler, we will still see Lock:Escalation events when the escalations are attempted, but by inspecting sys.dm_tran_locks, we can verify that only row locks are taken by the transaction.

Unfortunately, this technique could require keeping a transaction open indefinitely on the table (in those cases where a set time limit, such as the one hour used in Listing 5.2, may not be sufficient), even though no rows are locked. In addition, if that table has triggers or foreign keys referencing other tables, SQL Server may still escalate locks on the referenced tables, so preventing lock escalation on a single table may not be as simple as we might wish.

Using trace flags 1224 and 1211

In general, lock escalation does not cause immediate blocking problems. In fact, escalation cannot occur if it would cause an immediate conflict, as when another process has a lock on another row or page of the same resource. SQL Server will attempt to escalate a lock when it reaches any of the thresholds, but if there is a conflict, it will continue to acquire the individual locks, and keep trying to escalate the locks.

SQL Server provides two trace flags that can control lock escalation for an entire SQL Server instance.

- **Trace flag 1224** disables escalation due to exceeding the upper limit on the number of locks acquired for a statement, but escalation can still occur if the amount of memory used for locks exceeds the threshold.

- **Trace flag 1211** disables escalation in all cases. Be very careful if considering turning this trace flag on, as SQL Server could end up acquiring an enormous number of locks.

Troubleshooting Blocking

Blocking is usually the most troublesome issue that arises when dealing with a multi-user system. In fact, blocking doesn't just happen when tasks have conflicting requests for locks; it can also happen when there is contention on other resources, such as memory, I/O, or processor resources. However, due to the space limitations of this book, we'll only discuss blocking that occurs when one session requests a lock that is incompatible with one already held on the resource by another session. Please refer to Chapter 3, Table 3-1, to review the lock compatibility matrix, if you need a reminder of what locks are mutually compatible.

Detecting blocking problems

Brief periods of blocking may be normal in an active SQL Server system, depending upon the type of workload. However, when processes are blocked for extended periods of time, it can appear to end-users as if queries are running much more slowly.

We can have the best tuned queries in the world, but if they can't get the data they need because it is locked, it will appear as if the queries are very slow. Blocking may also be problematic when contention causes the overall throughput of the system to suffer because the blockers are preventing other tasks from completing in a timely manner.

SQL Server provides multiple tools for detecting lock-based blocking problems. In addition to metadata tools such as specific lock-related DMVs, there are counters available through **PerfMon**, and several tools, such as the **SQLDiag** utility, built on top of the DMVs and PerfMon counters.

We'll start at a high level, looking at ways to quickly detect whether or not blocking is a problem in a system, and then proceed to finding out what is causing the blocking, and resolving the problems.

PerfMon counters

We can use Performance Monitor (PerfMon) to determine, at a glance, whether locks being acquired on a SQL Server instance are causing blocking. The `Processes blocked` counter in the `SQLServer:General Statistics` object will show the number of blocked processes. We can then add counters such as the `Lock Waits` counter from the `SQLServer:Wait Statistics` object to determine the number of locks being held, and the duration of the locks. The Perfmon counters provide summary information only; that is, they allow us to determine whether or excessive blocking is a problem, but they don't tell us which processes are blocked or which processes are blocking.

DMVs

The `sys.dm_os_waiting_tasks` DMV returns a formatted list of all currently waiting tasks, along with the blocking task, if it is known. Table 5-1 has been adapted from SQL Server Books Online and summarizes the columns returned from `sys.dm_os_waiting_tasks`.

Column	Description
`waiting_task_address`	The waiting task's memory address, which allows us to distinguish multiple tasks within a session.
`session_id`	Can be used to join with `sys.dm_exec_requests`.
`exec_context_id`	Execution context id of the waiting task: 0 is the main or parent thread.
`wait_duration_ms`	The wait duration in milliseconds.
`wait_type`	The wait type of the current waiting task.
`resource_address`	Memory address of the resource for which the task is waiting. Use it to join with `sys.dm_tran_locks` on `lock_owner_address`.
`blocking_task_address`	The blocking task's memory address, if available.
`blocking_session_id`	Blocker's session id, if available. Negative integers -2, -3, -4 have special meaning and are explained below.
`blocking_exec_context_id`	Execution context id of the blocking task.
`resource_description`	Textual description of the resource on which the task is waiting.

Table 5-1: Columns available in `sys.dm_os_waiting_tasks`.

Note that `sys.dm_os_waiting_tasks` returns information at the task level, as opposed to the session level. If a query is running in parallel, and one of its threads is blocking or being blocked, `sys.dm_os_waiting_tasks` will reveal which thread (or task) is actually involved in the blocking.

There are some conditions where the `blocking_session_id` may not refer to an actual `session_id` value. As mentioned in the SQL Server Books Online discussion of `sys.dm_os_waiting_tasks`, sometimes the value of `blocking_session_id` may be `NULL` because there is no blocking session, or SQL Server cannot identify the blocking session. When inspecting lock-based blocking on a multi-user system, this should not be very common. However, SQL Server will sometimes report the `blocking_session_id` as a negative number. There are three possible codes for when the `session_id` might be negative.

- -2 – The locked resource is owned by an orphaned distributed transaction.

- -3 – The locked resource is owned by a deferred recovery transaction.

- -4 – For a latch wait, internal latch state transitions prevent identification of the session id.

Another nice feature is that `sys.dm_os_waiting_tasks` returns the duration of the wait, so that we can add filters to return only those rows relating to waits of a duration that is long enough to be of concern, i.e. the most likely causes of problematic blocking. For example, the query in Listing 5-3 will show only those waits that have been occurring for more than five seconds. The `sys.dm_os_waiting_tasks` view returns rows for system processes that are not actually waiting on a specific session, so I have also filtered the output to return only those waits where there actually is a blocking session.

In one session, we open a transaction and perform an `UPDATE` on the `SalesOrderDetail` table in the `AdventureWorks` database. In a second session, we attempt to read rows that we know are locked, hence causing blocking. In a third session, we investigate the blocking by querying `sys.dm_os_waiting_tasks`.

```
USE AdventureWorks
GO
-- Connection 1
BEGIN TRAN
UPDATE   Sales.SalesOrderDetail
SET      OrderQty = OrderQty + 1
WHERE    SalesOrderID = 51100
         AND SalesOrderDetailID = 35974;
-- do not commit this transaction yet

-- Connection 2
SELECT   *
FROM     Sales.SalesOrderDetail
WHERE    SalesOrderID = 51100
         AND SalesOrderDetailID = 35974;
-- this query will block

-- Connection 3
SELECT   W.session_id AS waiting_session_id ,
         W.waiting_task_address ,
         W.wait_duration_ms ,
         W.wait_type ,
         W.blocking_session_id ,
         W.resource_description
FROM     sys.dm_os_waiting_tasks AS W
WHERE    W.wait_duration_ms > 5000
         AND blocking_session_id IS NOT NULL;
```

Listing 5-3: Examine the sys.dm_os_waiting_tasks DMV.

When reviewing the results, notice that the resource_description column contains a concatenated set of strings with information about the blocking session. In our example, the query in the second session is blocked on a row in the Sales.SalesOrderDetail table of the AdventureWorks database, and the resource_description column contains the information below, concatenated into a single string.

- `keylock`

- `hobtid=72057594080854016`

- `dbid=5`

- `id=lock800e0f80`

- `mode=X`

- `associatedObjectId=72057594080854016`

This information tells us that the type of lock is a key lock, the database id is 5, and the *blocking* session has an exclusive lock granted. The **sys.dm_os_waiting_tasks** DMV will report all waiting tasks, whether they are waiting for locks or not. Some of the waiting may have more to do with I/O or memory contention.

To refine our focus to just lock-based blocking we can use the **sys.dm_tran_locks** DMV, which returns information about all locks, not just the ones involved with blocking. This view returns a large number of columns and can potentially return thousands, or tens of thousands, of rows. The query in Listing 5-4 returns a subset of the columns and shows all of the locks that are in a **WAIT** state.

```
SELECT   L.resource_type ,
         DB_NAME(L.resource_database_id) AS DatabaseName ,
         L.resource_associated_entity_id ,
         L.request_session_id ,
         L.request_mode ,
         L.request_status
FROM     sys.dm_tran_locks AS L
WHERE    L.request_status = 'WAIT'
ORDER BY DatabaseName ,
         L.request_session_id ASC;
```

Listing 5-4:   Query to return all locks in a **WAIT** state.

It might be more convenient to see just the waiting locks and the granted locks on which they are waiting. When a requested lock is waiting, it will be waiting on the same resource that the blocking process has already locked. The `sys.dm_tran_locks` DMV uses both the `resource_associated_entity_id` along with the `resource_description` to identify the locked resource, so we use those columns to join the view with itself and just return rows for the blocked and blocking locks, as shown in Listing 5-5.

```
SELECT  L1.resource_type ,
        DB_NAME(L1.resource_database_id) AS DatabaseName ,
        L1.resource_associated_entity_id ,
        L1.request_session_id ,
        L1.request_mode ,
        L1.request_status
FROM    sys.dm_tran_locks AS L1
        JOIN sys.dm_tran_locks AS L2
                ON L1.resource_associated_entity_id =
                    L2.resource_associated_entity_id
                AND L1.request_status <> L2.request_status
                AND ( L1.resource_description = L2.resource_description
                    OR ( L1.resource_description IS NULL
                        AND L2.resource_description IS NULL
                        )
                    )
ORDER BY L1.request_status ASC;
```

Listing 5-5:   Query to return all locks in a WAIT state and the locks on which they are waiting.

In Listing 5-5, we join the `sys.dm_tran_locks` view to itself, and return all locks that have a different request status (picking out GRANT and WAIT status values), but the same `resource_associated_entity_id` (for example, the same table), and the same `resource_description`, or where `resource_description` is NULL in each case (to cover cases in which there is no `resource_description`).

Figure 5-1 shows my results (assuming the blocking from Listing 5-2 is still in effect).

	resource_type	DatabaseName	resource_associated_entity_id	request_session_id	request_mode	request_status
1	KEY	AdventureWorks	72057594080854016	55	X	GRANT
2	KEY	AdventureWorks	72057594080854016	57	S	WAIT

Figure 5-1: Output showing the waiting lock and the lock for which it is waiting.

Listing 5-5 returns only the ID for the `resource_associated_entity_id`. Listing 5-6 takes this a step further and decodes the `resource_associated_entity_id` by looking it up in the `sys.partitions` catalog view. The subquery passes the found `object_id` value to the `OBJECT_NAME` function. However, because the `sys.partitions` catalog view reports data per database, the inner `CASE` expression limits the subquery to returning values for just the current database, when the `resource_associated_entity_id` is not `DATABASE` or `OBJECT`. We will have to run this query in each database in question to get all the object names.

```
USE AdventureWorks
GO
SELECT  L1.resource_type ,
        DB_NAME(L1.resource_database_id) AS DatabaseName ,
        CASE L1.resource_type
          WHEN 'OBJECT'
          THEN OBJECT_NAME(L1.resource_associated_entity_id,
                           L1.resource_database_id)
          WHEN 'DATABASE' THEN 'DATABASE'
          ELSE CASE WHEN L1.resource_database_id = DB_ID()
                    THEN ( SELECT   OBJECT_NAME(object_id,
                                            L1.resource_database_id)
                           FROM     sys.partitions
                           WHERE    hobt_id =
                                    L1.resource_associated_entity_id
                         )
                    ELSE NULL
               END
        END AS ObjectName ,
        L1.resource_description ,
        L1.request_session_id ,
        L1.request_mode ,
        L1.request_status
```

```
FROM      sys.dm_tran_locks AS L1
          JOIN sys.dm_tran_locks AS L2
                  ON L1.resource_associated_entity_id =
                      L2.resource_associated_entity_id
WHERE     L1.request_status <> L2.request_status
          AND ( L1.resource_description = L2.resource_description
              OR ( L1.resource_description IS NULL
                  AND L2.resource_description IS NULL
                  )
              )
ORDER BY L1.resource_database_id ,
         L1.resource_associated_entity_id ,
         L1.request_status ASC;
```

Listing 5-6:   Query to return all locks in a WAIT state and the locks they are waiting on, including database and object names.

Note that the sys.dm_tran_locks DMV contains database id, resource type, and locking information that is not available from the sys.dm_os_waiting_tasks DMV. On the other hand, the sys.dm_tran_locks DMV does not return the length of time the blocking has been occurring. To get all this information from a single query, we can join the two DMVs together, as we'll see in the next section.

Finding the cause of blocking

Whenever sessions compete for locked resources, we may observe lock-based blocking. It is not always enough just to know the objects that are locked, but it can sometimes point us in the right direction. To get to the root of the blocking problem, however, we will most likely need to know the queries involved. Having identified the session_id of a blocked or blocking session, there is other metadata available to help us determine which query the blocking session is currently executing.

The Blocked Process Report

SQL Server provides an XML report called the **Blocked Process Report** that we can generate by running SQL Trace and electing to see the event in the *Errors and Warnings* category. In addition, we must previously have configured the option called **Blocked Process Threshold** to a number of seconds greater than 0. Having taken both these steps, every time a process is blocked for longer than the configured number of seconds, the trace will capture an event that contains an XML report in the `TextData` column. This report will show the query text for both the blocking and the blocked processes. This is by far the most straightforward method of finding the queries, but it may not always be convenient to use SQL Trace.

Getting the query text from the DMVs

In cases where we can't use SQL Trace, we can use the tools that SQL Trace uses behind the scenes, namely the the `sys.dm_os_waiting_tasks` and `sys.dm_tran_locks` DMVs and, with a little extra work, extract the relevant queries.

We'll create this query in two steps. First, we'll join the two DMVs to get the best information from each. Then we'll add subqueries to extract the query text.

In Listing 5-7, we can join the DMVs on the waiting task's `resource_address` from `sys.dm_os_waiting_tasks`, and the `lock_owner_address` in `sys.dm_tran_locks`.

```
SELECT   T.session_id AS waiting_session_id ,
         DB_NAME(L.resource_database_id) AS DatabaseName ,
         T.wait_duration_ms / 60000. AS Duration_in_minutes ,
         T.waiting_task_address ,
         L.request_mode ,
         L.resource_type ,
         L.resource_associated_entity_id ,
         L.resource_description AS lock_resource_description ,
         T.wait_type ,
         T.blocking_session_id ,
         T.resource_description AS blocking_resource_description
```

```
FROM    sys.dm_os_waiting_tasks AS T
        JOIN sys.dm_tran_locks AS L ON T.resource_address = L.lock_owner_address
WHERE   T.wait_duration_ms > 5000
        AND T.session_id > 50;
```

Listing 5-7: Joining the sys.dm_os_waiting_tasks and sys.dm_tran_locks DMVs.

In Listing 5-7, the results are paired, using sys.dm_os_waiting_tasks as the base table: the waiting session is listed with its task information, and then the locking information for the waiting task from sys.dm_tran_locks is added. The last columns contain information about the blocking session, again from sys.dm_os_waiting_tasks.

Now we can go to the second step and get the actual query text for each session. We can add a subquery that joins the **sys.dm_exec_requests** DMV and the **sys.dm_exec_sql_text()** function, and correlates that join back to the waiting task's **session_id**, to give us the query text. The complete query is shown in Listing 5-8.

```
SELECT  T.session_id AS waiting_session_id ,
        DB_NAME(L.resource_database_id) AS DatabaseName ,
        T.wait_duration_ms / 60000. AS duration_in_minutes ,
        T.waiting_task_address ,
        L.request_mode ,
        ( SELECT SUBSTRING(Q.text, ( R.statement_start_offset / 2 ) + 1,
                            ( ( CASE R.statement_end_offset
                                    WHEN -1 THEN DATALENGTH(Q.text)
                                    ELSE R.statement_end_offset
                                END - R.statement_start_offset ) / 2 ) + 1)
          FROM      sys.dm_exec_requests AS R
                    CROSS APPLY sys.dm_exec_sql_text(R.sql_handle) AS Q
          WHERE     R.session_id = L.request_session_id
        ) AS waiting_query_text ,
        L.resource_type ,
        L.resource_associated_entity_id ,
        T.wait_type ,
        T.blocking_session_id ,
        T.resource_description AS blocking_resource_description ,
```

```
        CASE WHEN T.blocking_session_id > 0
             THEN ( SELECT  ST2.text
                    FROM    sys.sysprocesses AS P
                    CROSS APPLY
                            sys.dm_exec_sql_text(P.sql_handle) AS ST2
                    WHERE   P.spid = T.blocking_session_id
                  )
             ELSE NULL
        END AS blocking_query_text
FROM    sys.dm_os_waiting_tasks AS T
        JOIN sys.dm_tran_locks AS L
              ON T.resource_address = L.lock_owner_address
WHERE   T.wait_duration_ms > 5000
        AND T.session_id > 50;
```

Listing 5-8:   Query to return the blocked processes and the queries they are running.

For more details on how the **sys.dm_exec_query_text** function is used, please see the description of that function in the Books Online.

Resolving blocking problems

Once we know the queries involved, the locked resource, and the type of locks involved, we can address the issue of how to resolve the blocking. As discussed previously, lock-based blocking problems may be caused by writers blocking writers, readers blocking writers, or writers blocking readers. Each type of blocking has its own potential solutions.

Killing a session

The easiest way to resolve a blocking situation is to kill one of the sessions, using the **KILL** command. Sometimes this is the best solution in an emergency, or for terminating an ad hoc query that really should not even be running on a production system. In some cases, however, killing one of the sessions might cause unexpected harm to the applications accessing the database. If a particular blocking process is a long-running

UPDATE or DELETE operation, then killing the session will cause a transaction rollback and the locks will not be released, nor the blocking problem resolved, until the rollback is finished, which will not usually happen immediately. In such cases, we may need to look for a better solution, by trying to find and fix the root cause of the blocking.

Resolving writer/writer blocking

There are not a lot of options for resolving writer/writer blocking in SQL Server because exclusive locks are always required by sessions that are modifying data. When two sessions both need to change the same data, and therefore both sessions need to acquire exclusive locks on the same resource, we may need to rewrite the transactions, or change the way that we run them, if we want to avoid the blocking problems. We can consider the options below.

Make data modification transactions shorter

One of the most effective methods for resolving problems with writers blocking writers is to make transactions shorter, where possible by including in each transaction only those statements that absolutely must succeed or fail as a unit. When a transaction causes SQL Server to acquire exclusive locks, it holds them until the transaction ends. Therefore, by reducing the duration of the transaction, we also reduce the time that the exclusive locks are required.

Reduce the number of locks taken by writers

Earlier, we discussed how reducing the batch sizes of bulk modifications processes could eliminate lock escalation, and the same technique can help reduce blocking. We might also try to separate the contending writers by running them at different scheduled times, such as moving bulk load operations to a period with low system usage.

Resolving reader/writer blocking

There are more options available to us for resolving reader/writer blocking in SQL Server, primarily because we can adjust the isolation level of the transactions involved, in order to reduce the number of shared locks required by readers (or simply stop shared locks being taken by readers). We can consider the following options.

Lower the isolation level to READ UNCOMMITTED

Prior to SQL Server 2005, one of the most common methods of resolving reader/writer blocking was to lower the isolation level, either by setting the reader's isolation level to READ UNCOMMITTED or placing a NOLOCK hint on the reader's query. As a result, SQL Server won't acquire shared locks for SELECT statements.

This will remove blocking issues but there are significant risks attached to the method. First of all, the lack of shared locks means that SELECT statements can, and will, read uncommitted data. In a system where few if any transactions are ever rolled back, that may mean the risk is very low. However, a query might read a newly-inserted row from a header table but not see any of the detail table rows that have not yet been inserted. For critical queries that must return accurate aggregations or calculations based on consistent committed data, reading uncommitted data will not be acceptable.

In addition, there is a small risk that a SELECT statement using a NOLOCK hint, or READ UNCOMMITTED isolation level, can fail. This can occur if SQL Server attempts to read a page that has been deleted, but where the DELETE operation is not complete and committed. The page might be accessible using the NOLOCK hint, but may lack the proper links to continue traversing the linked list and finish reading the required pages.

When this occurs, we'll see Error 601, and the query will abort. The text of Error 601 is: *Could not continue scan with NOLOCK due to data movement.*

It is not common to see this error, but if an application uses NOLOCK hints for READ UNCOMMITTED, it should test for this error and resubmit the query if it occurs. However, that's not the only possible problem with NOLOCK. It is possible for SELECT statements using the NOLOCK hint or READ UNCOMMITTED isolation level to skip rows resulting from page splits that occurred while the SELECT was under way. This can occur when SQL Server chooses an allocation scan to scan a table for a SELECT statement, and page splits occur that put new pages into an earlier part of the allocation map. The SELECT statement only reads the allocation table forward, and will therefore miss such pages. Conversely, the SELECT statement may read rows twice due to page splits, if a page that has already been read is split, and the new page is added into a part of the allocation map that hasn't yet been read.

Check for the correct isolation level

It's possible that some transactions will be using a more restrictive isolation level, REPEATABLE READ or SERIALIZABLE, when it is unnecessary. In some cases, developers may accidentally use one of these isolation levels when they do not really need it.

Lowering these isolation levels to the default READ COMMITTED will allow SQL Server to keep shared locks for a shorter time, releasing them before the transaction ends. The **Blocked Process Report** XML output file's isolation-level column reports the isolation level of each transaction. Range locks involved in the blocking indicate the transaction is using the SERIALIZABLE isolation level.

Use one of the snapshot-based isolation levels

As of SQL Server 2005, we can avoid the problems associated with reading uncommitted data by using one of the snapshot-based isolation levels. By far the easiest and most direct method is to change the way the default READ COMMITTED isolation level works, by setting READ_COMMITTED_SNAPSHOT ON for the target database.

This changes the way SELECT statements read committed data; instead of blocking when encountering an exclusive lock, they read prior versions of any data that has been changed. This option is not without its costs, and we'll cover details of how the snapshot-based isolation levels work in the next chapter.

Separate readers from writers

For longer-term solutions, we may want to consider separating any problematic reader queries (often long-running reports) from the writer queries. Sometimes this is called "separating reads from writes," but that phrase is an oversimplification because often only a subset of all the reader queries can be redirected to a read-only copy of the database.

Often, even in the most active OLTP databases, read activity greatly exceeds write activity. A majority of those reads may be able to read the data from another server or database. Creating a reporting server separate from the main server, and fed data by transactional replication (for example), may allow us to offload many of the problematic reader queries. Unfortunately those same queries may attempt to lock the same data that replication stored procedures are updating, so we may still need to apply READ_COMMITTED_SNAPSHOT to the subscriber database in order to eliminate the contention.

Another method for separating readers from writers would be to create a database snapshot of the current database on the SQL Server instance, a snapshot that has data current as of a specified time. The SELECT statements run against a database snapshot (which is read-only) will not acquire as many shared locks as they would on a read-write database.

Sometimes the most problematic reader queries are also those that need up-to-the-second data, so it's not possible to separate the conflicting readers from the writers. In that case, one of the snapshot-based isolation levels may be the best option.

Troubleshooting Deadlocking

A deadlock occurs when two sessions are each waiting for a resource that the other session has locked, and neither one can continue because the other is preventing it from gaining access to the required resource. A true deadlock is a Catch-22 in which, without intervention, neither session can ever make progress. When a deadlock occurs, SQL Server intervenes automatically. In this section, I'll refer mainly to deadlocks acquired due to conflicting locks, although deadlocks can also be detected on worker threads, memory, parallel query resources, and MARS resources.

Note that a simple wait for a lock is *not* a deadlock. When the process that's holding the lock completes, the waiting process gets the lock. Lock waits are normal, expected, and necessary in multi-user systems.

Types of deadlock

In SQL Server, two main types of deadlock can occur: a **cycle deadlock** and a **conversion deadlock**. Figure 5-2, taken from the SQL Server Books Online, shows an example of a cycle deadlock. Transaction 1 starts, acquires an exclusive table lock on the `Supplier` table, and requests an exclusive table lock on the `Part` table. Simultaneously, Transaction 2 starts, acquires an exclusive lock on the `Part` table, and requests an exclusive lock on the `Supplier` table. The two transactions become deadlocked – caught in a "deadly embrace." Each transaction holds a resource needed by the other process. Neither can proceed and, without intervention, both would be stuck in deadlock forever.

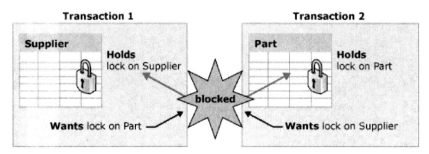

Figure 5-2:   A cycle deadlock.

We can generate a cycle deadlock using SQL Server Management Studio, and the script in Listing 5-9. We'll use the `Production.Product` table instead of `Part`, and `Purchasing.PurchaseOrderDetail` table instead of `Supplier`.

```
USE AdventureWorks
-- On one connection, start Transaction 1:
BEGIN TRAN
UPDATE    Purchasing.PurchaseOrderDetail
SET       OrderQty = OrderQty + 200
WHERE     ProductID = 922
          AND PurchaseOrderID = 499;
GO


-- Open a second connection, and start Transaction 2:
BEGIN TRAN
UPDATE    Production.Product
SET       ListPrice = ListPrice * 0.9
WHERE     ProductID = 922;
GO


-- Go back to the first connection, and execute this update statement:
UPDATE    Production.Product
SET       ListPrice = ListPrice * 1.1
WHERE     ProductID = 922;
GO
-- At this point, this first connection should block.
-- It is not deadlocked yet, however.  It is waiting for a lock
-- on the Production.Product table, and there is no reason
-- to suspect that it won't eventually get that lock.
```

```
--   Now go back to the second connection,
--   and execute this update statement:
UPDATE   Purchasing.PurchaseOrderDetail
SET      OrderQty = OrderQty - 200
WHERE    ProductID = 922
         AND PurchaseOrderID = 499;
GO
-- At this point a deadlock occurs.
```

Listing 5-9:   Generating a cycle deadlock.

The first connection will never get its requested lock on the `Production.Product` table because the second connection will not give it up until it gets a lock on the `Purchasing.PurchaseOrderDetail` table. Because the first connection already has the lock on the `Purchasing.PurchaseOrderDetail` able, we have a deadlock. One of the processes will receive the following error message. (Of course, the actual process ID reported will probably be different.)

```
Msg 1205, Level 13, State 51, Line 1
Transaction (Process ID 57) was deadlocked on lock resources with another process
and has been chosen as the deadlock victim. Rerun the transaction.
```

Figure 5-3 shows an example of a conversion deadlock. Process A and Process B both hold a shared lock on the same page. Each process wants to convert its shared lock to an exclusive lock but cannot do so because of the other process's lock. Again, intervention is required.

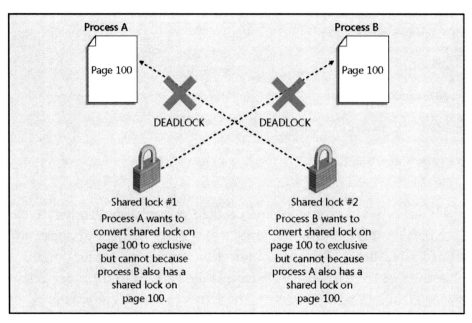

Figure 5-3:   A conversion deadlock.

Automatic deadlock detection

SQL Server automatically detects deadlocks and intervenes through the lock manager, which provides deadlock detection for locks. A separate thread, called LOCK_MONITOR checks the system for deadlocks every 5 seconds. As deadlocks occur, the deadlock detection interval is reduced and can go as low as 100 milliseconds. In fact, rather than wait for the next deadlock detection interval, the first few lock requests that cannot be satisfied, after a deadlock has been detected, will immediately trigger a deadlock search. If the deadlock frequency declines, the interval reverts to every 5 seconds.

This LOCK_MONITOR thread checks for deadlocks by inspecting the list of waiting locks for any *cycles*, which indicate a circular relationship between processes holding locks and processes waiting for locks. SQL Server attempts to choose, as the deadlock victim, the process that would be least expensive to roll back, considering the amount of work the process has already done. That process is killed and is sent **error message 1205**. The transaction is rolled back, meaning all its locks are released, so other processes involved in the deadlock can proceed. However, certain operations are marked as "golden," or unkillable, and cannot be chosen as the deadlock victim. For example, a transaction in the process of being rolled back cannot be chosen as a deadlock victim because the changes being rolled back could be left in an indeterminate state, causing data corruption.

Using the `SET DEADLOCK_PRIORITY` statement, we can determine the priority given to a process should it be involved in a deadlock; the higher the priority, the less likely it is to be chosen as the victim. There are 21 different priority levels, from –10 to 10. The value `LOW` is equivalent to –5, `NORMAL` is 0, and `HIGH` is 5. If the sessions have different deadlock priorities, the session with the lowest deadlock priority is chosen as the deadlock victim. If both sessions have set the same deadlock priority, SQL Server selects as victim the session that is less expensive to roll back.

Finding the cause of deadlocks

As well as automatically detecting that a deadlock has occurred, SQL Server will also make available data to indicate the processes and queries involved in the deadlock, so that we can determine exactly *why* the deadlock happened.

To determine the cause of a deadlock, we need to know the resources involved and the types of locks acquired and requested. For this kind of information, SQL Server provides **Trace Flag 1222** (this flag supersedes 1204, which was frequently used in earlier versions of SQL Server.) With this flag enabled, SQL Server will provide output in the form of a deadlock graph, showing the executing statements for each session, at the time of the deadlock; these are the statements that were blocked and so formed the conflict or cycle that led to the deadlock.

To form a complete picture of what caused the deadlock, we also need to know which statements originally acquired the locks that are blocking the later statements. SQL Server does not automatically maintain a complete record of the history of all the statements executed by each process, so this information is not available through Trace Flag 1222. In order to find out the statements that took the initial locks on the resources that form the base of the conflict, we must run a SQL Trace that captures the history for each of the processes involved in the deadlock.

When we enable Trace Flag 1222, the output is sent to the SQL Server error log. We can use the SQL Server Management Studio Log Viewer to view the information, but the output is sorted starting with the most recent event, so it's basically upside down. The best way to read the 1222 output is to copy the error log somewhere else and then read it using a simple text viewer, such as Notepad. We can then trim out extraneous information, as well as time and date information, to isolate the output to only what relates to the deadlock we are investigating.

The 1222 output is in an XML-like format but does not comply with any XSD schema, so it cannot be read using a utility like XML Notepad. We can divide the Trace Flag 1222 XML output into three sections: the **deadlock victim**, the participant **processes**, and the **resources**. Let's look at some 1222 output, generated when the deadlock generated from Listing 5-9 occurs, after enabling Trace Flag 1222 as shown in Listing 5-10.

```
DBCC TRACEON(1222, -1);
GO
```

Listing 5-10: Enabling Trace Flag 1222.

There is a great deal of information returned, much of which looks very cryptic, so we'll just focus on the critical pieces.

Deadlock victim

The first section of the 1222 output identifies the victim of the deadlock by using an internal process name. This is useful when relating other information in the trace flag output, and determining what information is connected to the victim.

```
deadlock-list
  deadlock victim= process593048
```

Processes

The next section identifies the victim and survivor processes and contains the most voluminous information. In our example, the first process listed is the victim, which you can tell by the process id, but it might just as well have been the other process (i.e. the first process might be the survivor, not the victim).

```
        process-list
            process id=process593048 taskpriority=0 logused=248 waitresource=KEY:
13:72057594045661184 (3e75cd3a78e7) waittime=4091 ownerId=7381
transactionname=user_transaction lasttranstarted=2012-05-14T16:27:27.520
XDES=0x8414d950 lockMode=U schedulerid=3 kpid=7696 status=suspended spid=52
sbid=0 ecid=0 priority=0 trancount=2 lastbatchstarted=2012-05-14T16:27:57.300
lastbatchcompleted=2012-05-14T16:27:27.520 clientapp=Microsoft SQL Server
Management Studio - Query hostname=TENAR hostpid=9148 loginname=TENAR\Kalen
isolationlevel=read committed (2) xactid=7381 currentdb=13 lockTimeout=4294967295
clientoption1=671090784 clientoption2=390200
            executionStack
                frame procname=adhoc line=1 sqlhandle=0x020000004fbb092c29dceca676884294d
f83a6c4d191eec8
        (@1 int,@2 smallint,@3 smallint)UPDATE [Purchasing].[PurchaseOrderDetail] set
[OrderQty] = [OrderQty]-@1  WHERE [ProductID]=@2 AND [PurchaseOrderID]=@3
                frame procname=adhoc line=1 sqlhandle=0x02000000a63fcb0cdeaa5cafca251aa15
18ff286a8a78917
        UPDATE   Purchasing.PurchaseOrderDetail
        SET      OrderQty = OrderQty - 200
        WHERE    ProductID = 922
                 AND PurchaseOrderID = 499;
```

```
       inputbuf
   UPDATE   Purchasing.PurchaseOrderDetail
   SET      OrderQty = OrderQty - 200
   WHERE    ProductID = 922
            AND PurchaseOrderID = 499;
```

For the first process, `process593048`, there is a wealth of information, some of which you would expect, such as the wait resource, database id, the `spid` number, and the input buffer containing the statement executed which was blocked. However, we also get information about the transaction isolation level and the `sqlhandle` of the command that actually acquired the resource.

The next process listed has a somewhat similar output.

```
      process-list
        process id=process5934c8 taskpriority=0 logused=2176 waitresource=KEY:
  13:72057594044678144 (bd095ec17235) waittime=17491 ownerId=7180
  transactionname=user_transaction lasttranstarted=2012-05-14T16:27:17.970
  XDES=0x844f7950 lockMode=X schedulerid=3 kpid=3528 status=suspended spid=55
  sbid=0 ecid=0 priority=0 trancount=2 lastbatchstarted=2012-05-14T16:27:43.907
  lastbatchcompleted=2012-05-14T16:27:17.970 clientapp=Microsoft SQL Server
  Management Studio - Query hostname=TENAR hostpid=9148 loginname=TENAR\Kalen
  isolationlevel=read committed (2) xactid=7180 currentdb=13 lockTimeout=4294967295
  clientoption1=671090784 clientoption2=390200
        executionStack
          frame procname=adhoc line=1 stmtstart=58 sqlhandle=0x0200000040756627d058
  1021091c2bcb38bd70b4892954f4
      UPDATE [Production].[Product] set [ListPrice] = [ListPrice]*@1  WHERE
  [ProductID]=@2
          frame procname=adhoc line=1 sqlhandle=0x02000000288f20321de34ef8cb5d031cb
  9a00cb157ae7069
      UPDATE   Production.Product
      SET      ListPrice = ListPrice * 0.9
      WHERE    ProductID = 922;
        inputbuf
      UPDATE   Production.Product
      SET      ListPrice = ListPrice * 0.9
      WHERE    ProductID = 922;
```

Deadlocked resources

Lastly, the 1222 output lists the resources involved in the deadlock. This is the most readable portion of the output, and probably where it's best to focus.

```
    resource-list
      keylock hobtid=72057594045661184 dbid=13 objectname=AdventureWorks.
Purchasing.PurchaseOrderDetail indexname=PK_PurchaseOrderDetail_PurchaseOrderID_
PurchaseOrderDetailID id=lock8010c780 mode=X associatedObjectId=72057594045661184
        owner-list
          owner id=process5934c8 mode=X
        waiter-list
          waiter id=process593048 mode=U requestType=wait

      keylock hobtid=72057594044678144 dbid=13 objectname=AdventureWorks.
Production.Product indexname=PK_Product_ProductID id=lock82d75f00 mode=X associated
ObjectId=72057594044678144
        owner-list
          owner id=process593048 mode=X
        waiter-list
          waiter id=process5934c8 mode=X requestType=wait
```

In this case, if we know the structure of our tables, we would know that both indexes (PK_PurchaseOrderDetail_PurchaseOrderID_PurchaseOrderDetailID and PK_Product_ProductID) are clustered primary keys, so we know that a key lock refers to a row of the table. At a glance, you can tell that one process had an exclusive lock on a row in the AdventureWorks.Purchasing.PurchaseOrderDetail table, and the other process was waiting to get an update lock. At the same time, the other process had an exclusive lock on a row in the AdventureWorks.Production.Product table, and the first process is waiting to get an exclusive lock on it.

Table 5-2 summarizes the output from the deadlock graphs, which then exposes most of the causes of the deadlock.

Output	Victim	Survivor
Process id	process593048	process5934c8
Database	AdventureWorks	AdventureWorks
Resource Type	keylock	keylock
Resources	`AdventureWorks.Purchasing.Purcha-seOrderDetail.PK_PurchaseOrderDe-tail_PurchaseOrderID_PurchaseOr-derDetailID`	`AdventureWorks.Pro-duction.Product.PK_Product_ProductID`
Lock Granted	X	X
Lock Requested	U	X

Last Command	`UPDATE Purchasing.PurchaseOrderDe-tail`
	`SET OrderQty = OrderQty - 200`
	`WHERE ProductID = 922`
	`    AND PurchaseOrderID = 499;`
		`UPDATE Production.Product`
		`SET ListPrice = ListPrice`
		`* 0.9`
		`WHERE ProductID= 922;`

Table 5-2: A sample summary of the Trace Flag 1222 output.

Once we know the resources and the statements that conflicted on them, we often have enough information to diagnose and resolve the deadlock. In some cases, we may need to dig deeper to find out what statements acquired the locks on the resources to begin with, which will require running SQL Trace to get a full history for each transaction.

Note, again, that the output of Trace Flag 1222 in the SQL Server error log can be voluminous. It can help to recycle the error log (using the system stored procedure `sp_cycle_errorlog`) periodically and then save the error logs elsewhere, in order to isolate the deadlocks to be analyzed.

Minimizing deadlocks

Be aware that it is rarely possible to guarantee that deadlocks will never occur. Tuning for deadlocks primarily involves minimizing the likelihood of their occurrence. Most of the techniques for minimizing the occurrence of deadlocks are similar to the general techniques for minimizing blocking problems. However, there is one technique that is only applicable to avoiding deadlock situations. In the example in Figure 5-2, the cycle deadlock could have been avoided if the transactions had decided on a protocol beforehand – for example, if they had decided to always access the `Product` table first and the `PurchaseOrderDetail` table second. Then one of the transactions would get the initial exclusive (X) lock on the table first, and the other would wait for the lock to be released. One process waiting for a lock is normal and natural. Remember, waiting for a lock, even for a prolonged period, is not the same thing as a deadlock.

Always try to have a standard protocol for the order in which transactions access tables. If we know that a transaction might need to update the row after reading it, it should initially request an update (U) lock, not a shared (S) lock. If both transactions request a U lock, rather than a S lock, the transaction that is granted a U lock is assured that the lock can later be promoted to an X lock. The other transaction requesting a U lock has to wait. The use of a U lock serializes the requests for an X lock. Other transactions needing only to read the data can still get their S locks and read. The holder of the U lock is guaranteed an X lock, so the deadlock is avoided.

Although we cannot, generally speaking, avoid deadlocks completely, the impact on any users involved, and on the rest of the system, should be minimal if our applications handle deadlocks appropriately. Appropriate handling implies that when an Error 1205 occurs, the application resubmits the batch, which will most likely succeed on a second try. Once one session is killed, its transaction is aborted, and its locks are released, and the other session involved in the deadlock can finish its work and release its locks, so the environment will not be conducive to another deadlock.

Summary

In this chapter, we looked at various techniques for troubleshooting problems with SQL Server locking and blocking, focusing on the metadata available to track down the resources involved in a blocking situation. We also examined some uses for Performance Monitor and SQL Server trace flags. In addition to illustrating methods for tracking down the source of the blocking problems, we also discussed possible steps to resolve the problem, or to avoid the problems in the first place.

Chapter 6: Optimistic Concurrency

Throughout this book, we've focused mostly on the mechanisms of the pessimistic concurrency model, whereby SQL Server relies exclusively on locking to enforce the ACID-compliance of its transactions. In other words, in a pessimistic concurrency environment, locks are acquired in order to avoid read phenomena such as dirty reads, non-repeatable reads and phantom reads, depending on the required ANSI isolation level and, as a result, readers block writers and writers block readers.

However, the ANSI SQL definitions of each of the transaction isolation levels specify only which of the behaviors each level allows, not how to implement each isolation level. Under the optimistic concurrency model, enabled via snapshot-based isolation, SQL Server can prevent some or all of these read phenomena (depending on the mode of snapshot-based isolation in use) without the need to acquire locks, therefore greatly reducing blocking in the database.

In order to achieve this, optimistic concurrency uses a **row versioning** technique, whereby SQL Server stores in `tempdb` copies (versions) of all the previously committed versions of any data rows, since the beginning of the oldest open transaction (*i.e.* it keeps those copies as long as there are any transactions that might need to access them). The space in `tempdb` used to store previous versions of changed rows is the **version store**. When using this row versioning, readers do not block writers, and writers do not block readers (though writers do still take locks and will block other writers).

In this chapter, we'll discuss:

- row versioning and how it works

- snapshot-based isolation, the new modes of operation it introduces, snapshot isolation (SI) and read committed snapshot isolation (RCSI), and how they work

- the potential for update conflicts in SI mode

- monitoring and managing the version store – especially disk space usage.

Some people consider optimistic concurrency to be the ultimate troubleshooting technique to avoid most, though not all, blocking problems. While it's true that optimistic concurrency greatly reduces SQL Server's dependence on the use of locks to enforce ACID-compliance for its transactions, it does bring with it a whole new set of trouble-shooting techniques, and a few problematic issues. As such, I prefer to view it as simply an *alternative* way to handle concurrent database access.

Overview of Row Versioning

Before optimistic concurrency was introduced in SQL Server 2005, the only way to reduce blocking, and increase concurrency (without rewriting code) was to use READ UNCOMMITTED isolation, whereby readers are allowed to perform dirty reads (reading whatever data is there at the time, regardless of whether it's currently being updated) and so aren't blocked by writers. The downsides to this are clear and we've discussed them previously. If our results must always be based on committed data, we need to be willing to wait for changes to be committed.

With SQL Server 2005 and later, we have a better, optimistic alternative. In fact, two better options, in the form of the two flavors of snapshot-based isolation: snapshot isolation and a non-blocking flavor of READ COMMITTED isolation called "read committed snapshot isolation."

These snapshot-based isolation levels rely on **row versioning**, rather than locking, to prevent read phenomena. Row versioning works, as we'll discuss in more detail in the next section, by making any transaction that changes data store the old row versions in an area of tempdb called the version store. By keeping the old versions of the data around, a "snapshot" of the database (or a part of the database) can be constructed from these old versions. The term "snapshot" refers to the set of rows that are valid for the point in time of the operation being performed.

RCSI prevents dirty reads without the need for transactions to acquire shared locks when reading data. Instead of blocking when unable to acquire a shared lock, if a required database page is being modified, the reader retrieves, from the version store, the previously committed values of the set of rows it needs. In this case, it retrieves a snapshot of the data as it existed at the time the current *statement* started. RSCI does not prevent non-repeatable reads or phantoms.

Use of SI prevents dirty reads, non-repeatable reads, and phantom reads, again without the need for reading transactions to acquire locks; the readers simply retrieve a snapshot of the data, as it existed at the time the current *transaction* started.

This is the big difference between optimistic and pessimistic concurrency: with the former, writers and readers will not block each other. In other words, using locking terminology, a session requesting an exclusive lock will not block when another session is reading data in the requested resource and, conversely, a session trying to read data will not block when the requested resource currently has an exclusive lock.

In this way, system concurrency is increased. Note, however, that SQL Server still acquires locks during data modification operations, so writers will still block writers, and everything we've discussed previously about lock types, lock modes, and lock duration is still relevant to optimistic concurrency and row versioning.

In order for the row versioning mechanism to work correctly, SQL Server must keep old versions of any row that a transaction updates or deletes. If multiple updates are made to the same row, then multiple older versions of the row might need to be maintained, and these multiple older versions must be maintained for as long as there are any transactions that might need to access them. For these reasons, we often refer to row versioning as *multi-version concurrency control*.

As you can imagine, to support the storing of multiple older versions of rows in the version store may require a lot of additional disk space in the `tempdb` database. Just as all databases in a SQL Server instance share the `tempdb` database, all databases that use row versioning share the same space in the version store.

In addition, we cannot set a maximum or minimum size for the version store; all space in the `tempdb` database is available for use by any process, in any database that needs `tempdb` space, for any reason, be it for user-defined temporary tables, system worktables, or the version store.

How Row Versioning Works

When we update a row in a table or index, the new row is marked with a value called the **transaction sequence number** (XSN) of the transaction that is doing the update. The XSN is a monotonically increasing number, which is unique within each SQL Server database. When updating a row, the previous version of the row is stored in the version store, and the new version of the row contains a pointer to the old version of the row in the version store. The new row also stores the XSN value, reflecting the time the row was modified.

Each old version of a row in the version store might, in turn, contain a pointer to an even older version of the same row. All the old versions of a particular row are chained together in a linked list, and SQL Server might need to follow several pointers in a list to reach the right version. The version store must retain versioned rows for as long as there are operations that might require them. As long as a transaction is open, all versions of rows that have been modified by that transaction must be kept in the version store, and version of rows read by a statement (RCSI) or transaction (SI) must be kept in the version store as long as that statement or transaction is open. In addition, the version store must also retain versions of rows modified by now-completed transactions if there are any older versions of the same rows.

In Figure 6-1, Transaction T3 generates the current version of the row, and it is stored in the normal data page. The previous versions of the row, generated by Transaction T2 and Transaction Tx, are stored in pages in the version store (in `tempdb`).

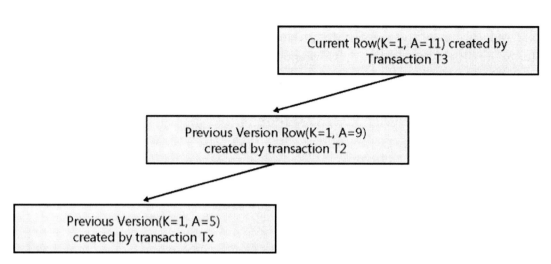

Figure 6-1: Versions of a row.

Before switching to a row-versioning-based isolation level, for reduced blocking and improved concurrency, we must carefully consider the tradeoffs. In addition to requiring extra management to monitor the increased use of tempdb for the version store, versioning slows the performance of UPDATE operations, due to the extra work involved in maintaining old versions. The same applies, to a much lesser extent, for DELETE operations, since the version store must maintain at most one older version of the deleted row.

Be aware that data modification operations will bear this cost, even if there are no current readers of the data. Once we configure a database to use one of the snapshot-based isolation levels, every UPDATE and DELETE operation will create a version. Any readers using row versioning will incur the extra cost of traversing the pointers to find the appropriate version of the requested row.

In addition, remember that the optimistic concurrency model of SI assumes (optimistically) that not many update conflicts will occur. As such, it may not be suited to cases where we expect many concurrent updates to the same rows.

Under snapshot-based isolation, writers don't block readers, but simultaneous writers are still not allowed. In the default pessimistic model, the first writer will block all subsequent writers but, using SNAPSHOT isolation, subsequent writers could receive error messages regarding update conflicts, and the application would need to resubmit the original request. For reasons that we'll discuss in a later section, these update conflicts will occur only when using SI, not with the enhanced read committed snapshot isolation level.

Snapshot-based Isolation Levels

As noted previously, SQL Server provides two types of snapshot-based isolation, both of which use row versioning to maintain the snapshot (the set of rows valid for the point in time the operation was performed):

- **read committed snapshot isolation (RCSI)** – queries return committed data as of the beginning of the current *statement*

- **snapshot isolation (SI)** – queries return committed data as of the beginning of the current *transaction*.

Enabling snapshot-based isolation

Let's first see how to enable each flavor, and then we'll examine how each one works.

Enabling RCSI

We enable and disable the first type, RCSI, with the ALTER DATABASE command, as shown in Listing 6-1.

```
ALTER DATABASE AdventureWorks
SET READ_COMMITTED_SNAPSHOT ON
```

Listing 6-1:   Enabling RCSI in the `AdventureWorks` database.

Once such a command has completed, no further changes are required, and RCSI will be the default isolation level for that database. Any transaction that would have operated under the default **READ COMMITTED** isolation will run under RCSI. Of course, we can change a connection to operate in another isolation level besides **READ COMMITTED**, but any **READ COMMITTED** transactions will operate using RCSI.

Ironically, for an isolation level intended to help avoid blocking, the **ALTER DATABASE** command in Listing 6-1 will block if there are any connections in the database other than the one issuing the command. Until the change is successful, the database continues to operate as if it is not in RCSI mode.

We can avoid the blocking by specifying a **TERMINATION** clause for the **ALTER** command, as shown in Listing 6-2.

```
ALTER DATABASE AdventureWorks
SET READ_COMMITTED_SNAPSHOT ON WITH NO_WAIT
```

Listing 6-2:   Enabling RCSI in the `AdventureWorks` database without blocking.

If there are any users in the database, rather than block, Listing 6-2 will fail with the following error:

```
Msg 5011, Level 14, State 5, Line 1
User does not have permission to alter database 'AdventureWorks', the database does
not exist, or the database is not in a state that allows access checks.
Msg 5069, Level 16, State 1, Line 1
ALTER DATABASE statement failed.
```

Alternatively, we could specify one of the ROLLBACK termination options, to kill any current database connections. For full details on the various termination options, please see the ALTER DATABASE command in Books Online.

Enabling SI

We must enable the second type of snapshot-based isolation, SI, in two places. First, we must enable it at the database level, just as for RCSI, using an ALTER DATABASE command such as that showing in Listing 6-3.

```
ALTER DATABASE AdventureWorks
SET ALLOW_SNAPSHOT_ISOLATION ON;
```

Listing 6-3: Enabling SI in the AdventureWorks database.

It must also be set at the session level, just as for any of the non-default ANSI levels, using SET TRANSACTION ISOLATION LEVEL SNAPSHOT.

When altering the database to allow SI, the presence of other connections will not necessarily block the command in Listing 6-3 but the presence of any active (i.e. data-modifying) transactions in the database, will block the ALTER DATABASE command. However, this does not mean that there is no effect until the statement completes. Changing the database to allow full SI can be a deferred operation. The database can actually be in one of four states with regard to ALLOW_SNAPSHOT_ISOLATION. It can be ON or OFF, but it can also be IN_TRANSITION_TO_ON or IN_TRANSITION_TO_OFF.

When we ALTER a database to ALLOW_SNAPSHOT_ISOLATION, SQL Server waits for the completion of all currently active transactions and in the meantime the database status is set to IN_TRANSITION_TO_ON. At this point, any new UPDATE or DELETE transactions will start generating versions in the version store.

During the transition period, we can open a new session, and execute the SET
TRANSACTION ISOLATION LEVEL SNAPSHOT command successfully, but no new
SNAPSHOT transactions can actually start until the transactions that were active when
we issued the ALTER DATABASE are complete. This is because any data modification
transactions that were already running at that time will *not* be storing row versions, as
the data is changed, so any new SI transactions would have no committed versions of the
data to read.

If we try to SELECT data in a SI session, while the database is still in a transition state, we
see the following error message:

```
Msg 3956, Level 16, State 1, Line 1
Snapshot isolation transaction failed to start in database 'AdventureWorks' because
the ALTER DATABASE command which enables snapshot isolation for this database has
not finished yet. The database is in transition to pending ON state. You must wait
until the ALTER DATABASE Command completes successfully.
```

As soon as all transactions have finished that were active when the ALTER command
began, the ALTER can finish and the state change will be complete. The database will now
be in the state ALLOW_SNAPSHOT_ISOLATION.

Taking the database out of ALLOW_SNAPSHOT_ISOLATION mode is similar and, again,
there is a transition phase.

- SQL Server waits for the completion of all active transactions, and the database status
  is set to IN_TRANSITION_TO_OFF.

- New snapshot transactions cannot start.

- Existing snapshot transactions still execute snapshot scans, reading from the
  version store.

- New transactions continue generating versions.

Working with RCSI

RCSI is a statement-level snapshot isolation, which means any queries will see the most recent committed values as of the beginning of the *statement* (as opposed to the beginning of the *transaction*). Remember that RCSI is just a non-locking variation of READ COMMITTED isolation, so there is no guarantee that read operations are repeatable.

The best way to understand what this means is to see it in action. Listing 6-4 shows two transactions running in the AdventureWorks database, which has been enabled for RCSI. Before either transaction starts running, the ListPrice value of Product 922 is 3.99.

Time	Transaction 1	Transaction 2
1	BEGIN TRAN UPDATE Production.Product SET ListPrice = 10.00 WHERE ProductID = 922;	BEGIN TRAN
2		SELECT ListPrice FROM Production.Product WHERE ProductID = 922; -- SQL Server returns 3.99
3	COMMIT TRAN	SELECT ListPrice FROM Production.Product WHERE ProductID = 922; -- SQL Server returns 10.00
4		COMMIT TRAN

Listing 6-4:   A SELECT running in RCSI.

We should note that at `Time = 2`, the change made by Transaction 1 is still uncommitted, so it still holds a lock on the row for `ProductID = 922`. However, Transaction 2 will not block on that lock; it will have access to an old version of the row with a last committed `ListPrice` value of 3.99. After Transaction 1 has committed and released its lock, Transaction 2 will see the new value of the `ListPrice`.

Again, keep in mind that RCSI is just a variation of the default isolation level `READ COMMITTED`. The same behaviors, indicated back in Table 1-1, are allowed and disallowed. In `READ COMMITTED` isolation, the only guarantee is that we won't read dirty (uncommitted) data. With *pessimistic* concurrency, SQL Server prevents us from reading the dirty data by locking it, and preventing other processes from reading that data, until the transaction commits or rolls back, and the data is no longer dirty. With *optimistic* concurrency, SQL Server prevents us from reading the dirty data by providing us with older versions of the data that were committed.

The biggest benefit of RCSI is that we can introduce greater concurrency because readers do not block writers and writers do not block readers. Don't forget that writers do still block writers, because the normal locking behavior applies to all `UPDATE`, `DELETE`, and `INSERT` operations. No `SET` options are required for any session to take advantage of RCSI, so we can reduce the concurrency impact of blocking and deadlocking without any change in our applications.

Working with SI

SI offers a transactionally consistent view of the data. Any data read will be the most recent committed version, as of the beginning of the *transaction*, rather than the statement. This prevents, not only dirty reads, but also non-repeatable reads and phantom reads. A key point to keep in mind is that the transaction does not start at the `BEGIN TRAN` statement; for the purposes of SI, a transaction starts the first time the transaction accesses any data in the database.

As an example of SI, let's revisit our example from the RCSI section, and see how the behavior differs. If you're going to run this example, make sure you set **READ_COMMITTED_SNAPSHOT** to OFF for the database. Listing 6-5 shows two transactions running in the AdventureWorks database, which has been enabled for SI by setting **ALLOW_SNAPSHOT_ISOLATION** to ON. Before either transaction starts running, the ListPrice value of Product 923 is 4.99.

Even though Transaction 1 has committed, Transaction 2 continues to return the initial value it read of 4.99, until Transaction 2 completes. Only after Transaction 2 is done, will the connection read a new value for ListPrice.

Time	Transaction 1	Transaction 2
1	BEGIN TRAN	
2	UPDATE Production.Product SET ListPrice = 10.00 WHERE ProductID = 923;	SET TRANSACTION ISOLATION LEVEL SNAPSHOT
3		BEGIN TRAN
4		SELECT ListPrice FROM Production.Product WHERE ProductID = 923; -- SQL Server returns 4.99 -- beginning of the -- transaction
5	COMMIT TRAN	

Time	Transaction 1	Transaction 2

6		`SELECT ListPrice`
		`FROM Production.Product`
		`WHERE ProductID  = 923;`
		`-- SQL Server returns 4.99`
		
		`-- Return the committed value`
		`-- as of the beginning of the`
		`-- transaction`

7		`COMMIT TRAN`

8		`SELECT ListPrice`
		`FROM Production.Product`
		`WHERE ProductID  = 923;`
		`-- SQL Server returns 10.00`

Listing 6-5: A SELECT running in a SNAPSHOT transaction.

Viewing database state

We can enable a database for SI and/or RCSI but enabling one does not automatically enable or disable the other. We enable or disable each one individually using separate ALTER DATABASE commands.

The catalog view `sys.databases` contains several columns that report on the snapshot isolation state of a database. The column `snapshot_isolation_state` has possible values of 0 to 4, indicating each of the four possible SI states, and the `snapshot_isolation_state_desc` column spells out the state. Table 6-1 summarizes what each state means.

Snapshot Isolation State	Description
OFF	SI is disabled in the database. In other words, transactions in snapshot isolation are not allowed. Database versioning state is initially set to OFF during recovery. If versioning is enabled, versioning state is set to ON after recovery.
IN_TRANSITION_TO_ON	The database is in the process of enabling SI. It waits for the completion of all update transactions that were active when the ALTER DATABASE command was issued. New update transactions in this database start paying the cost of versioning by generating row versions. Transactions under snapshot isolation cannot start.
ON	SI is enabled. New snapshot transactions can start in this database. Existing snapshot transactions (in another snapshot-enabled database) that start before versioning state is turned ON cannot do a snapshot scan in this database because the snapshot those transactions are interested in is not properly generated by the update transactions.
IN_TRANSITION_TO_OFF	The database is in the process of disabling the SI state and is unable to start new snapshot transactions. Update transactions still pay the cost of versioning in this database. Existing snapshot transactions can still do snapshot scans. IN_TRANSITION_TO_OFF does not become OFF until all existing transactions finish.

Table 6-1:   Possible values for database option ALLOW_SNAPSHOT_ISOLATION.

The is_read_committed_snapshot_on column has a value of 0 or 1. Table 6-2 summarizes what each state means.

READ_COMMITTED_SNAPSHOT	
State	**Description**
0	READ_COMMITTED_SNAPSHOT is disabled. Database versioning state is initially set to 0 during recovery. If READ_COMMITTED_SNAPSHOT was enabled in the database being recovered, after recovery the READ_COMMITTED_SNAPSHOT state is set to 1.
1	READ_COMMITTED_SNAPSHOT is enabled. Any query with READ COMMITTED isolation will execute in the non-blocking mode.

Table 6-2:   Possible values for the database option READ_COMMITTED_SNAPSHOT.

We can see the values of each of these snapshot states for all our databases with the query in Listing 6-6.

```
SELECT  name ,
        snapshot_isolation_state_desc ,
        is_read_committed_snapshot_on ,
        *
FROM    sys.databases
```

Listing 6-6:   Determining snapshot setting for all databases.

Update conflicts

One crucial difference between the two optimistic concurrency levels is that SI can potentially result in update conflicts when a process (such as a transaction that first reads data and then tries to update it) sees the same data for the duration of its transaction and is not blocked even though another process is changing the same data.

Time	Transaction 1	Transaction 2
1		SET TRANSACTION ISOLATION LEVEL SNAPSHOT
2		BEGIN TRAN
3		SELECT Quantity FROM Production.ProductInventory WHERE ProductID = 872; -- SQL Server returns 324 -- This is the beginning of -- the transaction
4	BEGIN TRAN UPDATE Production.ProductInventory SET Quantity=Quantity + 200 WHERE ProductID = 872; -- Quantity is now 524	
5		UPDATE Production.ProductInventory SET Quantity=Quantity + 300 WHERE ProductID = 872; -- Process will block

Time	Transaction 1	Transaction 2
6	`COMMIT TRAN`	
7		`-- Process will receive Error 3960`

Listing 6-7: An update conflict in snapshot isolation.

Listing 6-7 illustrates two transactions attempting to update the `Quantity` value of the same row in the `ProductInventory` table in the `AdventureWorks` database. Two clerks receive shipments of a product with `ProductID` 872, and attempt to update their inventory. The `AdventureWorks` database has `ALLOW_SNAPSHOT_ISOLATION` set to `ON`, and before either transaction starts, the `Quantity` value of Product 872 is 324.

The conflict happens because Transaction 2 started when the `Quantity` value was 324. When Transaction 1 updated that value, SQL Server saved the row version with a value of 324 in the version store. Transaction 2 will continue to read that row for the duration of the transaction. If SQL Server allowed both `UPDATE` operations to succeed, we would have a classic lost update situation. Transaction 1 added 200 to the quantity, and then Transaction 2 would add 300 to the original value and save that. The 200 added by Transaction 1 would be completely lost. SQL Server will not allow that.

When Transaction 2 first tries to do the `UPDATE`, it doesn't get an error immediately; it is simply blocked. Transaction 1 has an exclusive lock on the row, so when Transaction 2 attempts to get an exclusive lock, it is blocked. If Transaction 1 had rolled back its transaction, Transaction 2 would have been able to complete its `UPDATE`.

However, Transaction 1 committed, so SQL Server detects a conflict and generates the following error:

```
Msg 3960, Level 16, State 2, Line 1
Snapshot isolation transaction aborted due to update conflict. You cannot use
snapshot isolation to access table 'Production.ProductInventory' directly or
indirectly in database 'AdventureWorks' to update, delete, or insert the row that
has been modified or deleted by another transaction. Retry the transaction or
change the isolation level for the update/delete statement.
```

Conflicts are possible only with SI (and not with RCSI) because SI is transaction based, not statement based. If we executed the example in Listing 6-7 in a RCSI-enabled database, the UPDATE statement executed by Transaction 2 would not use the old value of the data. It would be blocked when trying to read the current Quantity and then, when Transaction 1 finished, it would read the new updated Quantity as the current value and add 300 to that. Neither update would be lost.

When working in SI, be aware that conflicts can happen. We can minimize their likelihood but, as with deadlocks, there is no guarantee that conflicts will never happen. We must write applications to handle conflicts appropriately, and not assume that the UPDATE has succeeded. If conflicts occur occasionally, consider it part of the price to pay for use of SI. If they occur too often, you might need to take extra steps.

If update conflicts are proving to be a problem, consider carefully whether SI is necessary for that database. If it is, determine whether the statement-based RCSI might offer the required behavior without the cost of detecting and dealing with conflicts.

If full SI really is required, then you might consider using the UPDLOCK query hint to prevent the conflicts. In our example, Transaction 2 could use UPDLOCK on its initial SELECT as shown in Listing 6-8.

```
SELECT   Quantity
FROM     Production.ProductInventory WITH ( UPDLOCK )
WHERE    ProductID = 872;
```

Listing 6-8: Using UPDLOCK to prevent update conflicts in SI.

The UPDLOCK hint will force SQL Server to acquire UPDATE locks for Transaction 2, on the selected row. When Transaction 1 then tries to update that row, it will block. It is not using SI, so it will not be able to see the previous value of Quantity. Transaction 2 can perform its UPDATE because Transaction 1 is blocked, and it will commit. Transaction 1 can then perform its UPDATE on the new value of Quantity, and neither UPDATE will be lost.

Summary of snapshot-based isolation levels

SI and RCSI are similar, in the sense that they are based on versioning of rows in a database. However, there are some key differences in how we enable these options from an administration perspective, and in how they affect our applications. We've discussed many of these differences already but, for completeness, Table 6-3 lists both the similarities and the differences between the two types of snapshot-based isolation.

SNAPSHOT	READ COMMITTED SNAPSHOT
The database must be configured to allow SI, and the session must issue the command SET TRANSACTION ISOLATION LEVEL SNAPSHOT.	The database must be configured to use RCSI, and sessions must use the default isolation level. No code changes are required.

SNAPSHOT	READ COMMITTED SNAPSHOT
Enabling SI for a database is an online operation. It allows the DBA to turn on versioning for one particular application, such as big reporting snapshot transactions, and turn off versioning after the reporting transaction has started to prevent new snapshot transactions from starting. Turning on SI state in an existing database is synchronous. When the `ALTER DATABASE` command is given, control does not return to the DBA until all existing update transactions that need to create versions in the current database finish. At this time, `ALLOW_SNAPSHOT_ISOLATION` is changed to `ON`. Only then can users start a snapshot transaction in that database. Turning off SI is also synchronous.	Enabling RCSI for a database requires an X lock on the database. All users must be kicked out of a database to enable this option.
There are no restrictions on active sessions in the database when this database option is enabled.	There should be no other sessions active in the database when you enable this option.
If an application runs a snapshot transaction that accesses tables from two databases, the DBA must turn on `ALLOW_SNAPSHOT_ISOLATION` in both databases before the application starts a snapshot transaction.	RCSI is really a table-level option, so the table from each database can have its own individual setting. One table might get its data from the version store, and the other table will be reading only the current versions of the data. There is no requirement that both databases must have the RCSI option enabled.

SNAPSHOT	READ COMMITTED SNAPSHOT
The IN_TRANSITION versioning states do not persist. Only the ON and OFF states are remembered on disk.	There are no IN_TRANSITION states here. Only ON and OFF states persist.
When a database is recovered after a server crash, shut down, restored, attached, or made ONLINE, all versioning history for that database is lost. If database versioning state is ON, we can allow new snapshot transactions to access the database, but we must prevent previous snapshot transactions from accessing the database. Those previous transactions are interested in a point in time before the database recovers.	N/A. This is an object-level option; it is not at the transaction level.
If the database is in the IN_TRANSITION_TO_ON state, ALTER DATABASE SET ALLOW_SNAPSHOT_ISOLATION OFF will wait for about 6 seconds and might fail if the database state is still in the IN_TRANSITION_TO_ON state. The DBA can retry the command after the database state changes to ON. This is because changing the database versioning state requires a U lock on the database, which is compatible with regular users of the database who get an S lock but not compatible with another DBA who already has a U lock to change the state of the database.	N/A. This option can be enabled only when there is no other active session in the database.

SNAPSHOT	READ COMMITTED SNAPSHOT
For read-only databases, versioning is automatically enabled. You still can use `ALTER DATABASE SET ALLOW_SNAPSHOT_ISOLATION ON` for a read-only database. If the database is made read-write later, versioning for the database is still enabled.	Similar.
If there are long-running transactions, a DBA might need to wait a long time before the versioning state change can finish. A DBA can cancel the wait, and versioning state will be rolled back and set to the previous one.	N/A.
You cannot use `ALTER DATABASE` to change database versioning state inside a user transaction.	Similar.
You can change the versioning state of `tempdb`. The versioning state of `tempdb` is preserved when SQL Server restarts, although the content of `tempdb` is not preserved.	You cannot turn this option `ON` for `tempdb`.
You can change the versioning state of the master database.	You cannot change this option for the master database.
You can change the versioning state of model. If versioning is enabled for model, every new database created will have versioning enabled as well. However, the versioning state of `tempdb` is not automatically enabled if you enable versioning for model.	Similar, except that there are no implications for `tempdb`.

SNAPSHOT	READ COMMITTED SNAPSHOT
You can turn this option ON **for msdb**.	You cannot turn on this option ON for msdb because this can potentially break the applications built on msdb that rely on blocking behavior of READ COMMITTED isolation.
A query in an SI transaction sees data that was committed before the start of the transaction, and each statement in the transaction sees the same set of committed changes.	A statement running in RCSI sees everything committed before the start of the statement. Each new statement in the transaction picks up the most recent committed changes.
SI can result in update conflicts that might cause a rollback or abort the transaction.	There is no possibility of update conflicts.

Table 6-3:   SNAPSHOT vs. READ COMMITTED SNAPSHOT isolation.

The Version Store

As soon as we enable a SQL Server database for ALLOW_SNAPSHOT_ISOLATION or READ_COMMITTED_SNAPSHOT, all UPDATE and DELETE operations start generating versions of the previously committed rows, and they store those row versions in the version store, on data pages in tempdb. SQL Server must retain version rows in the version store only as long as there are snapshot transactions and queries that might need them. SQL Server provides several DMVs that contain information about active snapshot transactions and the version store. We won't cover all the details of all of those DMVs, but we'll look at some of the crucial ones that can help us determine how much use is being made of the version store, and what snapshot transactions might be affecting the versions that need to be kept available.

The first DMV we'll look at, **sys.dm_tran_version_store**, contains information about the actual rows in the version store. Run the code in Listing 6-9 to make a copy of the **Production.Product** table, and then turn on **ALLOW_SNAPSHOT_ISOLATION** in the **AdventureWorks** database. Finally, verify that the option is **ON** and that there are currently no rows in the version store. Remember to close any active transactions currently using **AdventureWorks**.

```
USE AdventureWorks;
IF EXISTS ( SELECT  1
            FROM    sys.tables
            WHERE   name = 'NewProduct' )
    DROP TABLE NewProduct;
GO
SELECT  *
INTO    NewProduct
FROM    Production.Product;
GO
ALTER DATABASE ADVENTUREWORKS SET ALLOW_SNAPSHOT_ISOLATION ON;
GO
SELECT  name ,
        snapshot_isolation_state_desc ,
        is_read_committed_snapshot_on
FROM    sys.databases
WHERE   name = 'AdventureWorks';
GO
SELECT  COUNT(*)
FROM    sys.dm_tran_version_store
GO
```

Listing 6-9: Enabling a database for **SNAPSHOT** isolation.

Having verified that **ALLOW_SNAPSHOT_ISOLATION** is **ON** (and making sure **READ_COMMITTED_SNAPSHOT** is **OFF**) and there are no rows in the version store, we can proceed. Listing 6-10 runs a simple **UPDATE** statement on the **NewProduct** table and then re-examines the version store. What we should see is that, as soon as we enable **ALLOW_SNAPSHOT_ISOLATION**, SQL Server starts storing row versions, even if there are no snapshot transactions that need to read those versions.

```
UPDATE    NewProduct
SET       ListPrice = ListPrice * 1.1;
GO
SELECT    COUNT(*)
FROM      sys.dm_tran_version_store;
GO
```

Listing 6-10: Checking the version store after an update of data in an SI-enabled database.

We should now see 504 rows in the version store, because there are 504 rows in the `NewProduct` table. SQL Server writes to `tempdb` the previous version of each row, prior to the update.

Snapshot-based isolation and heavily updated databases

SQL Server starts generating versions in `tempdb` as soon as we enable a database for one of the snapshot-based isolation levels. In a heavily updated database, this can affect the behavior of other queries that use `tempdb`, as well as the server itself.

The version store maintains a linked list of previously committed versions of each row in the database. The current row points to the next older row, which can point to an older row, and so on. The end of the list is the oldest version of that particular row. To support row versioning, a row needs 14 additional bytes of overhead information: 8 bytes are for the pointer to the previous version of the row, and 6 bytes are to keep track of the XSN representing the time the row was modified. If a database is in a snapshot-based isolation level, all changes to both data and index rows must be versioned. A snapshot query traversing an index still needs access to index rows pointing to the older (versioned) rows. Therefore, in the index levels, we might have old values, as ghosts, existing simultaneously with the new value, and the indexes can require more storage space.

SQL Server will remove the extra 14 bytes of versioning information if we change the database to a non-snapshot isolation level. Having changed the database option, each time we update a row containing versioning information, SQL Server removes the versioning bytes.

Management of the version store

SQL Server manages the version store size automatically, and maintains a cleanup thread to make sure it does not keep versioned rows around longer than needed. For queries running under SI, the version store retains the row versions until the transaction that modified the data completes and the transactions containing any statements that reference the modified data complete. For **SELECT** statements running under RCSI, a particular row version is no longer required, and is removed, once the **SELECT** statement has executed.

SQL Server performs the regular cleanup function as a background process, which runs every minute and reclaims all reusable space from the version store. If **tempdb** actually runs out of free space, SQL Server calls the cleanup function and will increase the size of the files, assuming we configured the files for auto-grow. If the disk gets so full that the files cannot grow, SQL Server will stop generating versions. If that happens, any snapshot query that needs to read a version that was not generated due to space constraints will fail.

Although a full discussion of monitoring and troubleshooting the **tempdb** and the version store is beyond the scope of this book, note that more than a dozen performance counters can help, including counters to keep track of transactions that use row versioning. The counters below are contained in the **SQLServer:Transactions** performance object. SQL Server Books Online provides additional details and additional counters.

- **Free space in tempdb** – This counter monitors the amount of free space in the **tempdb** database. We can track this value to detect when **tempdb** is running out of space, which might lead to problems keeping all the necessary version rows.

- **Version store size** – This counter monitors the size in KB of the version store. Monitoring this counter can help determine a useful estimate of the additional space you might need for **tempdb**.

- **Version generation rate** and **version cleanup rate** – These counters monitor the rate at which space is acquired and released from the version store, in KB per second.

- **Update conflict ratio** – This counter monitors the ratio of update snapshot transactions that have update conflicts. It is the ratio of the number of conflicts compared to the total number of update snapshot transactions.

- **Longest transaction running time** – This counter monitors the longest running time in seconds of any transaction using row versioning. It can be used to determine whether any transaction is running for an unreasonable amount of time, as well as helping us to determine the maximum size needed in `tempdb` for the version store.

- **Snapshot transactions** – This counter monitors the total number of active snapshot transactions.

Snapshot transaction metadata

Besides `sys.dm_tran_version_store`, two other important DMVs for observing snapshot transaction behavior are `sys.dm_tran_transactions_snapshot`, and `sys.dm_tran_active_snapshot_database_transactions`.

All three of these views contain a column called `transaction_sequence_num`, which is the XSN discussed earlier. Each transaction is assigned a monotonically increasing XSN value when it starts a snapshot read, or when it writes data in a snapshot-enabled database. The XSN is reset to 0 when SQL Server is restarted. Transactions that do not generate version rows and do not use snapshot scans will not receive a XSN.

Another column, `transaction_id`, is also used in some of the snapshot transaction metadata. A transaction ID is a unique identification number assigned to the transaction. It is used primarily to identify the transaction in locking operations. However, it can also help us to identify which transactions are involved in snapshot operations. The transaction ID value is incremented for every transaction across the whole server, including internal system transactions so, regardless of whether or not that transaction is involved in any snapshot operations, the current transaction ID value is usually much larger than the current XSN.

We can check current transaction number information using the view `sys.dm_tran_current_transaction`, which returns a single row containing the columns below.

- **`transaction_id`** – Displays the transaction ID of the current transaction. When selecting from the view inside a user-defined transaction, we should continue to see the same `transaction_id` every time we select from the view. When running a `SELECT` from `sys.dm_tran_current_transaction` outside of a transaction, the `SELECT` itself will generate a new `transaction_id` value and a different value will be seen every time the same `SELECT` is executed, even in the same connection.

- **`transaction_sequence_num`** – The XSN of the current transaction, if it has one. Otherwise, this column returns 0.

- **`transaction_is_snapshot`** – Value is 1 if the current transaction was started under `SNAPSHOT` isolation; otherwise, it is 0. That is, this column will be 1 if the current session has explicitly issued `SET TRANSACTION ISOLATION LEVEL SNAPSHOT`.

- **`first_snapshot_sequence_num`** – When the current transaction started, it took a snapshot of all active transactions, and this value is the lowest XSN of the transactions in the snapshot.

- **`last_transaction_sequence_num`** – The most recent XSN generated by the system.

- **`first_useful_sequence_num`** – The upper bound (i.e. oldest) XSN of a transaction that is storing row versions. SQL Server need not retain in the version store any rows with an XSN less than this value.

In order to demonstrate how the values in the snapshot metadata are updated, we'll create a simple versioning scenario, as shown in Listing 6-11a. It will not provide a complete overview, but it will allow you to start exploring the versioning metadata for your own queries. The example uses the `AdventureWorks` database, which has `ALLOW_SNAPSHOT_ISOLATION` set to ON.

```sql
-- This is Connection 1
USE AdventureWorks;
GO
IF EXISTS ( SELECT  1
            FROM    sys.tables
            WHERE   name = 't1' )
    DROP TABLE t1;
GO
CREATE TABLE t1
    (
        col1 INT PRIMARY KEY ,
        col2 INT
    );
GO
INSERT  INTO t1
VALUES  ( 1, 10 ),
        ( 2, 20 ),
        ( 3, 30 );
GO
SET TRANSACTION ISOLATION LEVEL SNAPSHOT;
GO
BEGIN TRAN
SELECT  *
FROM    t1;
GO
SELECT  *
FROM    sys.dm_tran_current_transaction;
SELECT  *
FROM    sys.dm_tran_version_store;
SELECT  *
FROM    sys.dm_tran_transactions_snapshot;

-- The transaction is NOT committed or rolled back
```

Listing 6-11a: Examining metadata within a snapshot transaction.

The `sys.dm_tran_current_transaction` view should show something like this: the current transaction does have an XSN, and the transaction is a snapshot transaction. Also note that the `first_useful_sequence_num` value is the same as this transaction's XSN because currently there are no other valid snapshot transactions. Let's refer to this transaction's XSN as XSN1.

The version store should be empty (unless you've done other snapshot tests within the last minute). Also, `sys.dm_tran_transactions_snapshot` should be empty, indicating that there were no snapshot transactions that started while other transactions were still in progress.

Listing 6-11b starts a new connection (Connection 2), runs an UPDATE, and examines some of the metadata for the current transaction.

```
-- This is Connection 2:
BEGIN TRAN
GO
UPDATE   T1
SET      col2 = 100
WHERE    col1 = 1
SELECT   *
FROM     sys.dm_tran_current_transaction;
GO
```

Listing 6-11b: Start an UPDATE, running concurrently with the SNAPSHOT transaction from
Listing 6-11a, and examine the metadata.

Note that, although this second transaction has an XSN because it will generate versions, it is not running in SI, so the `transaction_is_snapshot` value is 0. We'll refer to this transaction's XSN as XSN2.

Listing 6-11c starts our third transaction (our second SNAPSHOT transaction), in Connection 3, to perform another SELECT (don't worry, this is the last one and we won't be keeping it around.) It will be almost identical to the first SELECT, but there will be an important difference in the metadata results.

```
-- This is Connection 3:
SET TRANSACTION ISOLATION LEVEL SNAPSHOT;
GO
BEGIN TRAN
SELECT  *
FROM    t1;
GO
SELECT  *
FROM    sys.dm_tran_current_transaction;
SELECT  *
FROM    sys.dm_tran_transactions_snapshot;
GO
```

Listing 6-11c: Examining metadata when a second SNAPSHOT transaction is running.

In the `sys.dm_tran_current_transaction` view, we'll see a new XSN for this transaction (XSN3), and that the value for `first_snapshot_sequence_num` and `first_useful_sequence_num` are both the same as XSN1. The query against the `sys.dm_tran_transactions_snapshot` view reveals that this transaction with XSN3 has two rows, indicating the two transactions that were active when this one started. Both XSN1 and XSN2 show up in the `snapshot_sequence_num` column.

We can now either COMMIT or ROLLBACK this transaction in Connection 3, and then close the connection. Having done so, go back to Connection 2, where we started the UPDATE, and COMMIT it. Now, go back to the first SELECT transaction in Connection 1 and rerun the SELECT statement (SELECT * FROM t1;), staying in the same transaction.

Even though the UPDATE in Connection 2 has committed, we will still see the original data values because we are running a SNAPSHOT transaction. We can examine the `sys.dm_tran_active_snapshot_database_transactions` view with the query in Listing 6-12.

```
SELECT  transaction_sequence_num ,
        commit_sequence_num ,
        is_snapshot ,
        session_id ,
        first_snapshot_sequence_num ,
        max_version_chain_traversed ,
        elapsed_time_seconds
FROM    sys.dm_tran_active_snapshot_database_transactions
```

Listing 6-12: Examining sys.dm_tran_active_snapshot_database_transactions.

The output is omitted, as it is too wide for the page, but there are many interesting columns returned. In particular, the transaction_sequence_num column contains XSN1, which is the XSN for the current connection. We could actually run this query from any connection; it shows *all* active snapshot transactions in the SQL Server instance and, because it includes the session_id, we can join it to sys.dm_exec_sessions to get information about the connection that is running the transaction, as shown in Listing 6-13.

```
SELECT  transaction_sequence_num ,
        commit_sequence_num ,
        is_snapshot ,
        t.session_id ,
        first_snapshot_sequence_num ,
        max_version_chain_traversed ,
        elapsed_time_seconds ,
        host_name ,
        login_name ,
        transaction_isolation_level
FROM    sys.dm_tran_active_snapshot_database_transactions t
        JOIN sys.dm_exec_sessions s ON t.session_id = s.session_id
```

Listing 6-13: Query to return information about active snapshot transactions and the sessions running those transactions.

Another column of note is `max_version_chain_traversed`. Although now its value should be 1, we can change that. Go back to Connection 2, in Listing 6-11b, and run the `UPDATE` statement shown in Listing 6-14 and then examine the version store to see the rows being added. Note that we use `BEGIN TRAN` and `COMMIT TRAN` for the `UPDATE`, even though they are not necessary for a single statement transaction, to make it clear that this transaction is complete.

```
BEGIN TRAN
UPDATE  T1
SET     col2 = 300
WHERE   col1 = 1
COMMIT TRAN;

SELECT  *
FROM    sys.dm_tran_version_store;
```

Listing 6-14: Querying the version store after a second `UPDATE`.

Return to Connection 1, run the same `SELECT` inside the original transaction and look again at the `max_version_chain_traversed` column in `sys.dm_tran_active_snapshot_database_transactions`. You should see that the number keeps growing. Repeated `UPDATE` operations, either in Connection 2 or in a new connection, will cause the `max_version_chain_traversed` value to keep increasing, as long as Connection 1 stays in the same transaction. Keep this in mind as an added cost of using snapshot isolation. As we perform more updates on data needed by snapshot transactions, our read operations will take longer because SQL Server will have to traverse a longer version chain to get the data needed by our transactions.

This is just the tip of the iceberg regarding how we can use the snapshot and transaction metadata to examine the behavior of our snapshot transactions.

Choosing a Concurrency Model

Pessimistic concurrency is the default in SQL Server 2005 and was the only choice in all earlier versions of SQL Server. Transactional behavior is guaranteed by locking, at the cost of greater blocking. When accessing the same data resources, readers can block writers and writers can block readers.

SQL Server was designed and built, initially, to use pessimistic concurrency. Therefore, we should consider using that model unless we can verify that optimistic concurrency really will work better for our applications. If we have an application where the cost of blocking is becoming excessive, and where many of the operations need to be performed in READ UNCOMMITTED isolation, optimistic concurrency is definitely worth considering.

> ### Warning: The NOLOCK *hint and RCSI*
>
> *If application code invokes* READ UNCOMMITTED *isolation by using the* NOLOCK *hint (or the equivalent* READUNCOMMITTED *hint), changing the database to RCSI will have no effect. The* NOLOCK *hint will override the database setting, and SQL Server will continue to read the uncommitted (dirty) data. The only solution is to update the code to remove the hints.*

In most situations, RCSI is recommended over SI for several reasons.

- RCSI consumes less `tempdb` space than SI.

- RCSI works with distributed transactions; SI does not.

- RCSI does not produce update conflicts.

- RCSI does not require any change in your applications. All that is needed is one change to the database options. Any of your applications written using the default READ COMMITTED isolation level will automatically use RCSI after making the change at the database level.

Use of SI can be considered in the following situations:

- The probability is low that any transactions will have to be rolled back because of an update conflict.

- Reports, based on long-running, multi-statement queries, need to be generated with point-in-time consistency. Snapshot isolation provides the benefit of repeatable reads without being blocked by concurrent modification operations.

Optimistic concurrency does have benefits, but also be aware of the costs. To summarize the benefits:

- `SELECT` operations do not acquire shared locks, so readers and writers will not block each other.

- All `SELECT` operations will retrieve a consistent snapshot of the data.

- The total number of locks needed is greatly reduced compared to pessimistic concurrency, so less system overhead is used.

- SQL Server will need to perform fewer lock escalations.

- Deadlocks will be less likely to occur.

When weighing concurrency options, we must consider the cost of the snapshot-based isolation levels.

- `SELECT` performance can be negatively affected when long-version chains must be scanned. The older the snapshot, the more time it will take to access the required row in an SI transaction.

- Row versioning requires additional resources in `tempdb`.

- Whenever either of the snapshot-based isolation levels is enabled for a database, `UPDATE` and `DELETE` operations must generate row versions. In general, `INSERT` operations do not generate row versions, but there are some cases where they might.

In particular, if we insert a row into a table with a unique index, then if there is an older version of the row with the same key value as the new row, and that old row still exists as a ghost, our new row will generate a version.

- Row versioning information increases the size of every affected row by 14 bytes.

- UPDATE performance might be slower due to the work involved in maintaining the row versions.

- If SQL Server detects a conflict, it may roll back an UPDATE operation that is using SI. We must program our applications to deal with any conflicts that occur.

- Carefully manage the space in tempdb. If there are very long-running transactions, SQL Server must retain in tempdb all the versions generated by UPDATE transactions during that time. If tempdb runs out of space, UPDATE operations won't fail, but SELECT operations that need to read versioned data might fail.

To maintain a production system using either of the snapshot-based isolation levels, be sure to allocate enough disk space for tempdb so that there is always at least 10 percent free space. If the free space falls below this threshold, system performance may suffer because SQL Server will expend more resources trying to reclaim space in the version store. The formula below provides a rough estimate of the size required by the version store.

[size of common version store] = 2 * [version store data generated per minute]
* [longest running time (minutes) of the transaction]

For long-running transactions, it might be useful to monitor the generation and cleanup rate using Performance Monitor, to estimate the maximum size needed.

Final Recommendations

Understand SQL Server's default behavior for managing concurrency.
Although I presented a number of different ways that we could override this default, 98% of the time it's best to let SQL Server handle the concurrency management. Having decided to use either pessimistic or optimistic concurrency, we should let SQL Server take it from there. This is probably the single most important thing we can do to troubleshoot concurrency problems.

Make sure your application developers know something about how SQL Server manages transactions.
Many blocking problems are the result of an application starting a transaction and then not processing the data quickly (e.g. due to reading the rows one at a time from the results) in order to terminate the transaction.

Understand the difference between blocking and waiting.
A process may be waiting for many things besides locks, and not every process holding onto locks is blocking another process. Get very familiar with the contents of the `sys.dm_exec_requests` and `sys.tran_tran_locks` views.

Understand the difference between blocking and deadlocking.
Although deadlocking usually sounds like a much more serious situation, because SQL Server handles it automatically, in most cases it has much less impact on total system throughput than blocking. If an application is coded to check for deadlock error message 1205 and respond appropriately, you may never experience any system problems from an occasional deadlock. However, make it a regular habit to monitor the number of deadlocks occurring, so you're aware when something changes.

Finally, practice using the monitoring tools even when you don't think you're having problems.

- Get used to watching the deadlock rate and average lock wait time using Performance Monitor.

- Check your error logs to see if any handled, unnoticed deadlocks have occurred (assuming you have Trace Flag 1222 enabled).

- Periodically look at `sys.dm_tran_locks` or run one of the blocking-report queries presented, just to see what is happening on your system.

The more we know of how our system behaves when things are going well, the quicker we'll spot problems, track them down and resolve them.

Index

A

B

C

D

E

O

SQL Server
and .NET Tools
from Red Gate Software

SQL Compare® Pro $595

Compare and synchronize SQL Server database schemas

↗ Eliminate mistakes migrating database changes from dev, to test, to production

↗ Speed up the deployment of new databse schema updates

↗ Find and fix errors caused by differences between databases

↗ Compare and synchronize within SSMS

> "Just purchased SQL Compare. With the productivity I'll get out of this tool, it's like buying time."
>
> **Robert Sondles** Blueberry Island Media Ltd

SQL Data Compare Pro $595

Compares and synchronizes SQL Server database contents

↗ Save time by automatically comparing and synchronizing your data

↗ Copy lookup data from development databases to staging or production

↗ Quickly fix problems by restoring damaged or missing data to a single row

↗ Compare and synchronize data within SSMS

> "We use SQL Data Compare daily and it has become an indispensable part of delivering our service to our customers. It has also streamlined our daily update process and cut back literally a good solid hour per day."
>
> **George Pantela** GPAnalysis.com

Visit **www.red-gate.com** for a 14-day, free trial

SQL Prompt Pro $295

Write, edit, and explore SQL effortlessly

- ⌐ Write SQL smoothly, with code-completion and SQL snippets
- ⌐ Reformat SQL to a preferred style
- ⌐ Keep databases tidy by finding invalid objects automatically
- ⌐ Save time and effort with script summaries, smart object renaming and more

> "SQL Prompt is hands-down one of the coolest applications I've used. Makes querying/developing so much easier and faster."
>
> **Jorge Segarra** University Community Hospital

SQL Source Control $295

Connect your existing source control system to SQL Server

- ⌐ Bring all the benefits of source control to your database
- ⌐ Source control schemas and data within SSMS, not with offline scripts
- ⌐ Connect your databases to TFS, SVN, SourceGear Vault, Vault Pro, Mercurial, Perforce, Git, Bazaar, and any source control system with a capable command line
- ⌐ Work with shared development databases, or individual copies
- ⌐ Track changes to follow who changed what, when, and why
- ⌐ Keep teams in sync with easy access to the latest database version
- ⌐ View database development history for easy retrieval of specific versions

> "After using SQL Source Control for several months, I wondered how I got by before. Highly recommended, it has paid for itself several times over."
>
> **Ben Ashley** Fast Floor

Visit **www.red-gate.com** for a 28-day, free trial

SQL Backup Pro

$795

Compress, encrypt, and strengthen SQL Server backups

- ↗ Compress SQL Server database backups by up to 95% for faster, smaller backups

- ↗ Protect your data with up to 256-bit AES encryption

- ↗ Strengthen your backups with network resilience to enable a fault-tolerant transfer of backups across flaky networks

- ↗ Control your backup activities through an intuitive interface, with powerful job management and an interactive timeline

> "SQL Backup is an amazing tool that lets us manage and monitor our backups in real time. Red Gate's SQL tools have saved us so much time and work that I am afraid my director will decide that we don't need a DBA anymore!"
>
> **Mike Poole** Database Administrator, Human Kinetics

SQL Monitor

from **$795**

SQL Server performance monitoring and alerting

↗ Intuitive overviews at global, cluster, machine, SQL Server, and database levels for up-to-the-minute performance data

↗ Use SQL Monitor's web UI to keep an eye on server performance in real time on desktop machines and mobile devices

↗ Intelligent SQL Server alerts via email and an alert inbox in the UI, so you know about problems first

↗ Comprehensive historical data, so you can go back in time to identify the source of a problem

↗ Generate reports via the UI or with Red Gate's free SSRS Reporting Pack

↗ View the top 10 expensive queries for an instance or database based on CPU usage, duration, and reads and writes

↗ PagerDuty integration for phone and SMS alerting

↗ Fast, simple installation and administration

> **"Being web based, SQL Monitor is readily available to you, wherever you may be on your network. You can check on your servers from almost any location, via most mobile devices that support a web browser."**
>
> **Jonathan Allen** Senior DBA, Careers South West Ltd

Visit **www.red-gate.com** for a 14-day, free trial

SQL Virtual Restore $495

Rapidly mount live, fully functional databases direct from backups

- ↗ Virtually restoring a backup requires significantly less time and space than a regular physical restore
- ↗ Databases mounted with SQL Virtual Restore are fully functional and support both read/write operations
- ↗ SQL Virtual Restore is ACID compliant and gives you access to full, transactionally consistent data, with all objects visible and available
- ↗ Use SQL Virtual Restore to recover objects, verify your backups with DBCC CHECKDB, create a storage-efficient copy of your production database, and more

> **"We find occasions where someone has deleted data accidentally or dropped an index, etc., and with SQL Virtual Restore we can mount last night's backup quickly and easily to get access to the data or the original schema. It even works with all our backups being encrypted. This takes any extra load off our production server. SQL Virtual Restore is a great product."**
> **Brent McCraken** Senior Database Administrator/Architect, Kiwibank Limited

SQL Storage Compress $1,595

Silent data compression to optimize SQL Server storage

- ↗ Reduce the storage footprint of live SQL Server databases by up to 90% to save on space and hardware costs
- ↗ Databases compressed with SQL Storage Compress are fully functional
- ↗ Prevent unauthorized access to your live databases with 256-bit AES encryption
- ↗ Integrates seamlessly with SQL Server and does not require any configuration changes

Visit **www.red-gate.com** for a 14-day, free trial

SQL Toolbelt

$1,995

The essential SQL Server tools for database professionals

You can buy our acclaimed SQL Server tools individually or bundled. Our most popular deal is the SQL Toolbelt: fourteen of our SQL Server tools in a single installer, with **a combined value of $5,930 but an actual price of $1,995**, a saving of 66%

Fully compatible with SQL Server 2000, 2005, and 2008

SQL Toolbelt contains:

↗ **SQL Compare Pro**

↗ **SQL Data Compare Pro**

↗ **SQL Source Control**

↗ **SQL Backup Pro**

↗ **SQL Monitor**

↗ **SQL Prompt Pro**

↗ **SQL Data Generator**

↗ **SQL Doc**

↗ **SQL Dependency Tracker**

↗ **SQL Packager**

↗ **SQL Multi Script Unlimited**

↗ **SQL Search**

↗ **SQL Comparison SDK**

↗ **SQL Object Level Recovery Native**

> **"The SQL Toolbelt provides tools that database developers, as well as DBAs, should not live without."**
>
> **William Van Orden** Senior Database Developer, Lockheed Martin

Visit **www.red-gate.com** for a 14-day, free trial

ANTS Memory Profiler　　　　$495

Find memory leaks and optimize memory usage

- ↗ Find memory leaks within minutes
- ↗ Jump straight to the heart of the problem with intelligent summary information, filtering options and visualizations
- ↗ Optimize the memory usage of your C# and VB.NET code

> "Freaking sweet! We have a known memory leak that took me about four hours to find using our current tool, so I fired up ANTS Memory Profiler and went at it like I didn't know the leak existed. Not only did I come to the conclusion much faster, but I found another one!"
>
> **Aaron Smith** IT Manager, R.C. Systems Inc.

ANTS Performance Profiler　　　　from $395

Profile your .NET code and boost the performance of your application

- ↗ Identify performance bottlenecks within minutes
- ↗ Drill down to slow lines of code thanks to line-level code timings
- ↗ Boost the performance of your .NET code
- ↗ Get the most complete picture of your application's performance with integrated SQL and File I/O profiling

> "ANTS Performance Profiler took us straight to the specific areas of our code which were the cause of our performance issues."
>
> **Terry Phillips** Sr Developer, Harley-Davidson Dealer Systems

> "Thanks to ANTS Performance Profiler, we were able to discover a performance hit in our serialization of XML that was fixed for a 10x performance increase."
>
> **Garret Spargo** Product Manager, AFHCAN

Visit **www.red-gate.com** for a 14-day, free trial

.NET Reflector ®   From $35

Decompile, browse, analyse and debug .NET code

- ↗ View, navigate and search through the class hierarchies of any .NET assembly,
     even if you don't have access to the source code
- ↗ Decompile and analyse any .NET assembly in C#, Visual Basic and IL
- ↗ Step straight into decompiled assemblies whilst debugging in Visual Studio, with the same debugging
     techniques you would use on your own code

> "One of the most useful, practical debugging tools that I have ever worked with in .NET! It provides complete browsing and debugging features for .NET assemblies, and has clean integration with Visual Studio."
>
> **Tom Baker** Consultant Software Engineer, EMC Corporation

> "EVERY DEVELOPER NEEDS THIS TOOL!"
>
> **Daniel Larson** Software Architect, NewsGator Technologies

SmartAssembly ®   from $795

.NET obfuscation, automated error reporting and feature usage reporting

- ↗ **Obfuscation:** Obfuscate your .NET code and protect your IP
- ↗ **Automated Error Reporting:** Get quick and automatic reports on exceptions your end-users
     encounter, and identify unforeseen bugs within hours or days of shipping; receive detailed reports
     containing a stack trace and values of the local variables, making debugging easier
- ↗ **Feature Usage Reporting:** Get insight into how your customers are using your application, rely on
     hard data to plan future development, and enhance your users' experience with your software

> "Knowing the frequency of problems (especially immediately after a release) is extremely helpful in prioritizing & triaging bugs that are reported internally. Additionally, by having the context of where those errors occurred, including debugging information, really gives you that leap forward to start troubleshooting and diagnosing the issue."
>
> **Ed Blankenship** Technical Lead and MVP

Visit **www.red-gate.com** for a 14-day, free trial

Performance Tuning with SQL Server Dynamic Management Views

Louis Davidson and Tim Ford

This is the book that will de-mystify the process of using Dynamic Management Views to collect the information you need to troubleshoot SQL Server problems. It will highlight the core techniques and "patterns" that you need to master, and will provide a core set of scripts that you can use and adapt for your own requirements.

ISBN: 978-1-906434-47-2
Published: October 2010

Defensive Database Programming

Alex Kuznetsov

Inside this book, you will find dozens of practical, defensive programming techniques that will improve the quality of your T-SQL code and increase its resilience and robustness.

ISBN: 978-1-906434-49-6
Published: June 2010

Brad's Sure Guide to
SQL Server Maintenance Plans
Brad McGehee

Brad's Sure Guide to SQL Server Maintenance Plans shows you how to use the Maintenance Plan Wizard and Designer to configure and schedule eleven core database maintenance tasks, ranging from integrity checks, to database backups, to index reorganizations and rebuilds.

ISBN: 978-1-906434-34-2
Published: December 2009

The Red Gate Guide to SQL Server
Team-based Development
Phil Factor, Grant Fritchey, Alex Kuznetsov, and Mladen Prajdić

This book shows how to use a mixture of home-grown scripts, native SQL Server tools, and tools from the Red Gate SQL Toolbelt, to successfully develop database applications in a team environment, and make database development as similar as possible to "normal" development.

ISBN: 978-1-906434-59-5
Published: November 2010

CPSIA information can be obtained at www.ICGtesting.com
Printed in the USA
LVOW111054240912

299896LV00003B/4/P